MATTHEW RITCHIE

MATTHEW RITCHIE

THE
TEMPTATION
OF THE
DIAGRAM

GETTY RESEARCH INSTITUTE
2017

CONTENTS

9 **Foreword**
Thomas W. Gaehtgens

10 **A Descent into the Diagram:
The Temptation of Matthew Ritchie**
Kenneth Rogers

30 **The Temptation of the Diagram**
Matthew Ritchie

130 **Schematic Aspects of an Aesthetics
of Diagrams**
Frederik Stjernfelt

143 **Afterword**
David Brafman

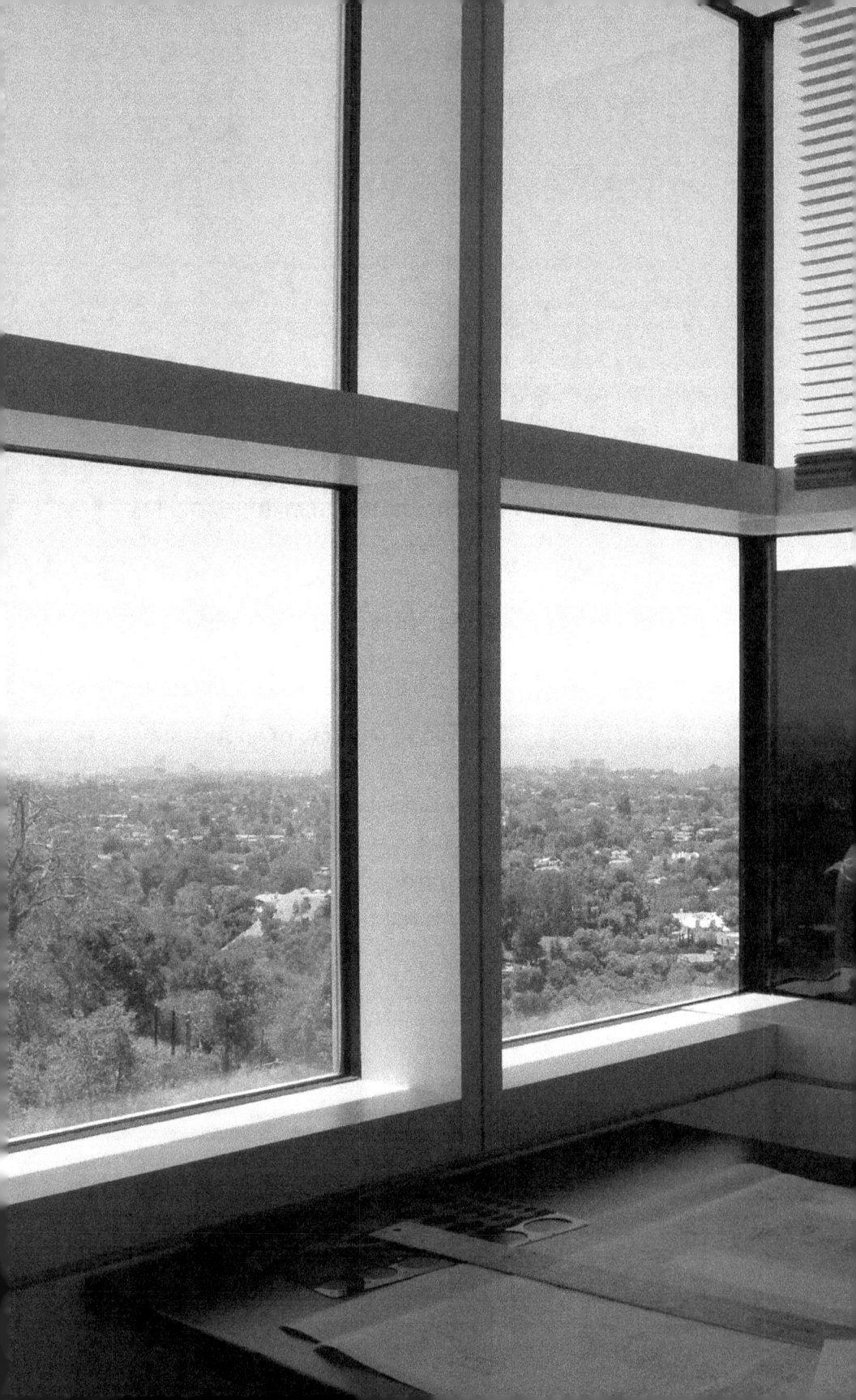

Previous spread: Matthew Ritchie, *The Temptation of the Diagram*, studio installation, Getty Research Institute, Los Angeles, 2012. Photo: Matthew Ritchie.

Foreword

When Matthew Ritchie occupied the studio of the artist in residence at the Getty Research Institute, the place was transformed into an astonishing *Gesamtkunstwerk*. The walls were covered with drawings of lines, graphics, and images to create an enigmatic network. The beholder was inspired and attracted at the same time to read and understand this pictorial diagram. But soon he realized that the symbols and letters were taken from mythological, astronomical, scientific books of which the GRI owns an abundant collection. The originality of this artist's oeuvre consists in visually mapping all the wonders and discoveries the world has to offer. He engages us visually and aesthetically in a subtle balance of seemingly logical, scientific expositions as well as creating an overwhelming poetic pictogram. This is the artist's dream, to explore and long for an understanding of the universe. Art and science are united in mysterious and cryptic infinity.

—Thomas W. Gaehtgens, *Director, Getty Research Institute*

A Descent into the Diagram:
The Temptation of Matthew Ritchie

Kenneth Rogers

I now began to watch, with a strange interest, the numerous things that floated in our company. I must have been delirious—for I even sought amusement in speculating upon the relative velocities of their several descents toward the foam below.

—Edgar Allan Poe, "A Descent into the Maelström" (1841)

I first met Matthew Ritchie at the Getty Research Institute (GRI) in January 2012 where he was the sole artist-in-residence among a diverse cohort of some twenty scholars. As a visual artist dropped into the heart of academe, Ritchie's perspective stood out among the rest, especially given that "artistic practice" was the annual research theme. I was already well familiar with Ritchie's art practice and knew him as the mischievous polymath who would take everything from quantum mechanics and string theory to literature and mythology and smash them together as if in the Hadron collider to see how they might splinter and corkscrew into unruly hybrid paintings, wall drawings, and multi-dimensional sculptures, both ordered and chaotic, but I knew nothing of his interest in diagrams. Although not a Getty scholar at the time, because my own research had brought me to the Getty I found myself regularly attending the program's many events and lectures held at the institute, and I had the good fortune of getting to know this group rather well. For those of us frequently at the GRI that spring, word gradually spread of an ambitious new installation Ritchie was assembling in his studio about diagrams. The lucky few who had caught a private glimpse would shake their head at a loss. "I can't explain it," they'd say, "you really have to see it to understand." I was intrigued.

As it so happened, there was a feedback diagram persistently reappearing in my ongoing research on attention and information aesthetics that was rolling around in my project like loose pebble stuck in my shoe—just when I thought the aggravation had gone, another version of the diagram would resurface again at the most inopportune moment. I lacked the basic means of confronting this stubborn and persistent problem; the diagram was the platform beneath everything about a key concept of attention, but I had no platform to understand the preconditions of the diagram itself. Over the winter months, I had several passing exchanges with Ritchie about his general art practice and his eclectic interests, and every conversation would inevitably turn back to the topic of diagrams, where he would offer keen insights on the subject and occasionally suggested a reading or two. When he spoke about diagrams, he was always alight with the focused passion of a scientist on the verge of a great breakthrough, as if his studio were a laboratory, and he were eagerly awaiting the results from the latest experiment before going back to recalibrate his instruments and run another cycle of tests. This was not so far from the truth. From these tantalizing, enigmatic glimpses into his project, my curiosity about the world of diagrams had now been thoroughly piqued, but not until my own visit to the studio later that spring did I fully understand the temptation.

My opportunity finally arrived in spring 2012 when, in lieu of delivering the customary lecture like the rest of the Getty cohort, Ritchie hosted a one-day open studio. One sunny afternoon a modest group of twenty or thirty visitors, largely made up of scholars and other GRI affiliates, were invited to roam his corner studio that flowed out onto a terrace boasting an implausibly dramatic vista with plunging views over the L.A. basin, where one could be easily lulled to daydream about the unknown destination of ships bound for the Pacific as they vanished stoically beyond the distant horizon. Inside, the view was no less arresting. The studio walls were flush with reproductions of hundreds upon hundreds of 8 ½ x 11-inch, black-and-white photocopies of diagrams. Wedged floor-to-ceiling, edge-to-edge in a makeshift grid, the installation included examples of every imaginable type: diagrams in the form of cartographies, charts, Venn sets, schemata, taxonomies, tables, graphs, dendrograms, rebuses, topologies, calendars, and mechanical drawings; diagrams representing the fields of physics, mathematics, cosmology, theology, psychology, biology, science, technology, linguistics, and the history of art; diagrams sourced from diverse geographic locations, cultures, and historical periods, from antiquity to the present. Diagrams from everywhere, appeared everywhere; en masse, the eclectic display stretched before us to completely dominate the entire visual field (see pp. 22–23).

The effect was a mesmerizing—an excess of shifting associations and bewildering juxtapositions magnified by the fact that, unless internal to a given diagram itself, each was mounted without caption or wall text of any kind. A dizzying scan across the room might take you from the concentric circles of Ptolemy's geocentric cosmology to the rectilinear quadrangular projections of Leon Battista Alberti's *De pictura* to the vertiginous fractals of the Mandelbrot set. Focusing on a localized area might leave you contrasting Freud's later topography of the unconscious to the schematic circuitry of Intel's breakthrough 386 processor. The catalog was so eclectic there appeared to be virtually no limiting parameters for inclusion into the collection but for one: each diagram, no matter how antiquated or arcane, was analogous to a formalized system of thought. At some time and place for a segment of human society, each was held up as a serious statement that proffered a specific epistemology or worldview, a statement sanctioned by institutional power and legitimized by formal knowledge. Like a modern day Diderot, Ritchie's installation was an audacious achievement of encyclopedic ambition nothing short of attempting the graphic encapsulation of the history of recorded knowledge through the diagrammatic form.

The already formidable aspiration of such undertaking only intensified when our cautious group was drawn in for a more careful inspection. Up close, our attention turned to a horizontal band of graph paper that scrolled along the entire length of the room, cutting directly through the midsection of the installation. Hand-scribed in fine print, Ritchie had assiduously taken an inventory of the entire contents of the visual display of diagrams above and below, which loosely functioned like an index or a reference guide. Organized by the dual factors of time and scale, the entries flowed linearly from left to right in a loose historical chronology and nonlinearly according to scale and frequency in a tangled web of crisscrossing lines and vectors. The entries cumulated into dense constellations and clusters of interlinked associations, whose oscillating patterns of free-scale correlation swarmed like starlings across the page. It was a master diagram, a diagram of diagrams, and it stood alone as the only bit of flotsam spit out of the visual maelstrom to help us paddle our way safely ashore.

Despite the sobering comprehensiveness of the enterprise, which might so easily have been levied upon us like some dreary and pedantic lecture, the encounter with Ritchie's installation felt refreshingly light, even whimsical. The whole wall fluttered with Scotch tape informality, and the sequence never appeared too careful or fixed in place. Each discrete example floated with the casual air of impermanence, no single diagram too precious to earn immunity from being unceremoniously swapped for one of the hundreds more unsorted examples stacked in brimming boxes on a studio tabletop in the far corner. The whole room felt ephemeral, improvised, like a throwaway sketch in mid-flight to the wastepaper basket, a mere trial before the artist ripped it up and set out to start the task all over again.

This sense of the temporary transformed the formidable into the approachable, and finding reassurance that there was no inflexible paradigm of the diagram bearing down on us, our once timid group was emboldened. We were unleashed into the space with errant curiosity, free to indulge in open exploration and savor the pleasures of infinite digression formed at the knife's edge between chance and order. It created a social space among us as well; we talked aloud, noting common observations and sharing startling discoveries, inspecting the walls for both the familiar and the peculiar, speculating on possible connections and then discarding these hypotheses for others. We relished the weirdness of it all. The walls were tempting us to decipher the overall system, and fragments of meaning strung together by ties of weak correlation dangled like bait. Once we had acclimated, the overall effect was a feeling of inhabiting diagrammatic space, of being inside a speculative machine for making sense of the disparate kinds of environments and objects that populate the unfamiliar and changing realities of contemporary life, all while never violating the feeling of improvisatory lightness. What made this sense of lightness all the more remarkable is that it was never achieved at the expense of content and history. Though the patchwork of diagrams was undeniably a thing of beauty to behold, it would have been all too easy for Ritchie to reduce the entire project to a decorative one-liner, effacing the diagram's significance into a superficial morphology of aesthetic forms—a succession of visual motifs and styles divorced from their historical and material frames of reference to become the modish equivalent of conceptual wallpaper. It may have felt temporary and light, but it was neither arbitrary nor insubstantial.

As both a work of art and research creation, the installation felt poised at the cusp of demonstrating some important principles about the source of a diagram's power. At a certain level, it could have stood as a critical comment on the problem of how to work with the notion of epistemic space after the post-linguistic turn, which has made recourse to ideas like discourse, paradigm, and episteme a largely inadequate way of grappling with new materialisms and the physicalization of information. As a corrective to this, the installation might have been putting forth the diagram as a path to reconcile the impasse between theories of representation and those of ontology. But the piece was too playful to be stamped with such a tidy theoretical template. It seemed as though the artist was almost toying with us by manufacturing the simulacra of theoretical cohesion that could not help but leave one to wonder about the perverse motivations underlying artistic invention: the mandala-like attention to detail and the prodigious expenditure of labor that walked the forlorn border between the obsessive and the absurd. How trustworthy was the framework Ritchie laid out? Why this order and not another? Who on earth could meaningfully link so many discrete things? Why on earth would anyone want to? From the profound weirdness of the experience, it would be easy to read the installation as the disordered symptom of an obsession. How quickly the heroic unwavering dedication to a singular problem can flip over to the Janus-faced obverse of eccentricity, fixation, and paranoia. Squint your eyes and this could have been a system of self-actualization created by an imperious autocrat leading an invented religious cult, or one might have conjured the cinematic cliché of the conspiracy-obsessed loner scrawling semi-legible rants about the illuminati on thumbtacked scraps of tattered evidence linked centripetally by uneven spokes of colored yarn.

These glib caricatures are not without a more serious precedent in the recent art historical record. When conspiracy aesthetics in studio art practice surged in the post-9/11 aughts, it relied heavily on the diagram as a means of visualizing the hidden machinations of power, in what critic Brian Holmes, remarking on the tendency, has called "energy diagrams" and "cartographies of excess." Mark Lombardi's prescient diagrams traced the corrupt, nepotistic liaisons among the highest echelons of government, finance, and industry to illustrate how this elite social network was organized into a global syndicate that could monopolize economic and geopolitical power. The Bureau d'Etude's ongoing series of "cartogrammes" all diagram the imbalanced organizational flow of intersecting world systems from governance, to finance, to global media conglomerates, to technologies of the self that together epitomize the equivalent of what Greg Elmer and Matthew Tiessen have described as the "neoliberal diagram." And Futurefarmer Josh On's open-ended web-based project "They Rule"(2004) is an interactive map diagraming all the affiliations of each member on the board of directors of all the major Fortune 500 companies, as a way of unveiling ruling-class oligopolies and the revolving door collusion between public and private sectors.

Ritchie's use of diagrams might easily be mistaken as work in the same vein as the above tradition, in that it does link together many statements and individuals who were, and are, invested with great social and political influence, but this superficial resemblance ends here. The aesthetic of conspiracy is always guided by an explicit theory and lays out hierarchical terms of power and exclusion. *The Temptation of the Diagram* does neither. Ritchie's method is far too inscrutable, his delivery far too deadpan. If there is any role he inhabits, it is more that of the trickster than the paranoid, and his project thus operates in quite the opposite way from the examples above. Rather than use the diagram as the privileged tool to lay bare a thesis about an order of power and domination, Ritchie puts forward the decoy of a great meta-system, like a ruse that entices us to pursue the tantalizing promise of a profound and definitive meaning. It is only when this promise inevitably falls short, and the system bows under the stress of its own ontological errors, that the master diagram begins to take over and we are left, finally, to consider what is generalizable about the diagrammatic writ large as a techno-social condition. Ritchie is less interested in the diagram of power than in the power of the diagram. If one can say that the concern of power shows up in his work, it is the power that inheres in the diagram itself because of its endlessly adaptable social function.

When mounted together like this and situated in relationship to every other example, each diagram in the collection was liberated from its own particular burden to analogize the world according to a value system ascribed from within the diagram itself. Ritchie's studio installation circumvented a given diagram's internal logic and reordered its epistemic position according to its cofunctioning with other diagrams and the shared history of their use. They were all still diagrams, of course, but diagrams at the moment of their becoming something else, a transformation delivered by their own collective reorganization around their own conditions of possibility. Through this elegant recursive method, Ritchie had brought eidetic diagrammatic reasoning as a way to understand the history of the diagram as a malleable epistemological figure especially equipped to foster a way of knowing and acting upon the world, and this is why *The Temptation of the Diagram* stands alone in the diagrammatic turn in contemporary art.

I left the installation transformed, sensitized. Diagrams had been completely invisible to me, but after a single afternoon in Ritchie's studio, I since cannot help but see their presence everywhere. Meteorological diagrams indicate global wind streams and ocean currents. Metro maps and international airport floor plans make the labyrinthine mega-architectures of modern transportation navigable at a glance. Infographics like population maps, pie charts, and bar graphs proliferate in trade publications, magazines, educational textbooks, and business reports. And the ever-present GUI (Graphical User Interface) is an interactive computational diagram that appears on all screen-based media to help organize our distributed digital lives. Crucial diagrams can have a collective impact or become the signature of a key concept or paradigm shift that can send ripples through the social body, as the Penrose diagram of Minkowski's space-time continuum did for post-Newtonian theoretical physics when it made the complicated mathematical and scientific abstraction of objects like black holes and gravity broadly accessible to the nonspecialist. Network diagrams can track and manage hyperobjects of staggering density, such as the distribution human genetic markers common to a large segment of the population or the infrastructure of the Internet, while common functional diagrams like a simple classroom seating chart or the pictorial assembly instructions included with an Ikea bookshelf aid us through the most routine of daily tasks. Aesthetic diagrams can open our ears to the meter of a poem, make visible the visual structure behind a painting, or help us intuit the lived-rhythm of a dance to convey what seems most human about human culture. But in examples that are no less significant, diagrams also record the minutia of the fictional and the frivolous, as in the elaborate tree diagram wiki of the entire ensemble the popular book and television series *Game of Thrones*, collectively recording every detail of interfamilial conquest with the unsurpassed ardor of fandom. Diagrams prosaic and popular, recondite and recherché, have imperceptibly spread throughout every branch of knowledge and quietly crept into every human endeavor to become an omnipresent and indispensible feature of everyday life. Yet given the surface fact of their ubiquity, arguably unparalleled at any other time in human history, why is it that we so seldom take notice of how they inhabit our world? Why does the diagram itself as either abstract model or historical form remain so remote and obscured from view?

While the diagram is a historical form, it has no formal historiography—no cataloged history of examples and cases that offer a consensus about what diagrams are and how and when they came about. When compared to visual art, music, or language, each of which has an entire discipline devoted to its study, the historical understanding of diagrams offers us precious little and is mostly relegated to the footnotes of philosophy, logic, rhetoric, linguistics, and critical theory. At first, it might seem correct to consider the diagram as another categorical subset of the visual image and thus to ground an explanation of its contemporary proliferation by way of extension, as simply another effect of the general twentieth-century explosion of mass visual culture. The problem with this tack is that diagrams function under a general rubric that is distinctively set apart from the history of images. For one thing, diagrams also function like language, in that they involve forms of symbolic representation. Further, unlike images, diagrams aren't merely illustrations that portray the world; they are also instruments that enable us to reason and act within it and upon it. They are utilitarian: they help us get from one place to the next, master an idea, understand a workflow, or feel our way through a new environment. We recognize and appreciate their enabling effect—along with the fascination they can unlock and the passions they can incite—but we rarely think about the diagram itself, and it often blends unnoticed into the opaque background of the worlds it has brought forth.

Without a doubt, diagrams do put things on visual display, but they also consist of information and transmit forms of rationality. This alignment with instrumental reason puts the diagram, at least since the Enlightenment, squarely within the history of science, as much as it is surely a part of the history of language, art, and visual culture. They are instruments constructed to posit hypotheses, test and retest ideas, arrive at discoveries and conclusions, and convert those results into pragmatic action. We draw on them for practical ends, often out of bare necessity of managing the diversification of tasks demanded of us in advanced technological societies. If the diagram is a visual form, that visual form is in the service of it becoming a platform for (if not quite a "paradigm" of) knowledge—it can determine how we know things and the things it makes knowable. But the knowledge it conveys is rarely general and almost always functionally discrete—adaptable to interact with some immediate set of unattained goals and circumstances or a specific lived environment. This makes it nearly impossible to arrive at the diagram itself as an empty form by dissociating it from the context of an individual case. Despite the best efforts of the academy to pin down the diagram in abstraction, one can only get so far with a sweeping historiography of forms, a categorical taxonomy of types, a unified theory, or a singular science of its functioning—a diagrammatology. The very fact that the diagram is expert at making other things known is what makes it so difficult to render it as knowable, in itself. Perhaps we so seldom take notice of how diagrams inhabit our world because we already unwittingly inhabit theirs. What would it mean to finally turn to face the diagram itself? How might we begin to move toward such a dangerous but alluring temptation?

The present volume takes a monumental step forward in developing a platform for understanding the diagram by forging an alternative path to methods of categorical abstractions that have repeatedly proved it a stubborn and elusive object of study. As a culmination of Ritchie's ongoing project, this iteration of *The Temptation of the Diagram* is an important refinement of a ongoing quest since its inception, and the occasion of this publication is a powerful consolidation of years of work produced across a variety formats, each tunneling toward the same problem with a different tool: the original open studio installation at the Getty Research Institute (2012), a roundtable workshop at the Getty Research Institute (2012), the multivolume publication of visual handbooks (2012–14), both a solo and a curated group exhibition at the Andrea Rosen Gallery, New York (2013 and 2014), a lecture series sponsored by the Andrew W. Mellon Foundation and hosted at Columbia University (2014)—all grouped together under the same name (see pp. 24–29). If this version is not necessarily the definitive statement, it is most certainly the definitive object. This latest iteration of Ritchie's sustained engagement with the diagram is the most concise, refined, and elegant visualization of the problem to date. The limited edition publication includes a sequence of 816 individual historical diagrams dated from antiquity to the present, all scaled down to fit forty-eight diagrams per 24 x 18-inch page and printed on thick, translucent paper stock that unfolds accordion-style into seventeen contiguous sheets that together form one single diagram over twenty-five-and-a-half feet across. The entire collection of diagrams is networked together according to chronology and function by an intricate linear drawing. Even in miniature, each individual diagram is fully legible on its own, but printed in opacity a striking gestalt emerges. From certain vantage points, the individual diagrams dissolve into stochastic background noise, and the network drawing jumps into the foreground, asserting its figural dominance over the content of the diagrams themselves. This parallel perceptual and conceptual pivot that alternates between the diagram's legibility and visibility is reinforced by the publication's material construction. Like an ancient codex, the work may be left in its case to be perused front-to-back, folio style, across a centerfold that divides recto and verso pages. Alternatively, the work can be unfolded and extended to a length of twenty-five and a half feet on a wall or across long table, enabling Ritchie's master diagram to be visually apprehended in its entirety.

    Ritchie's project is unprecedented in both method and historical scope. While cautiously avoiding the authoritative declaration of a universal theory, science, taxonomy, or systematization, this work still presents one of the richest catalogs of diagrams ever assembled, and offers penetrating insights into parallel and divergent paths in the polyvalent history of systems of thought. What makes his approach exceptional is that the method of understanding is analogical to its object. For a viewer to approach the master diagram and make it intelligible, she must do so by performing an individual act of diagrammatic reasoning, one that may never reach the same conclusion twice, but will always irrespectively reveal something about how the diagram performs itself. In interviews and his own writings, Ritchie has revealed the disparate influences and alliances he has forged for his own precarious descent into the diagrammatic field. While Frederik Stjernfelt's Peircean semiotic ontology of the diagram, Graham Harman's diagrammatic mutualism in the quadruple object, and Foucault and Deleuze's diagrammatic topologies of force relations together do the critical theory heavy lifting, Ritchie tempers these brittle treatises with the elasticity of examples from philosophy, literature, art, and myth that carefully reflect upon the productive failure of any encyclopedic and comprehensive will to knowledge. Standing out among many such examples are Diderot's *Encyclopédie*, the naively optimistic embodiment of the ethos of Enlightenment freethinking in a "Systematic Dictionary of the Sciences, Arts, and Crafts," and Gustav Flaubert's befittingly unfinished work of nineteenth-century satirical fiction, *Bouvard and Pécuchet*, in which two dilettantish antiheroes retreat to survey all the world's knowledge only to cynically renounce the gesture and return to their work as copy clerks at a custom desk built for two. Fact or fiction, both examples are equally emblematic of the hubris and folly involved in any attempt to grasp and systematize the universe of human knowledge. And, of course, Flaubert's rendition of *The Temptation of Saint Anthony*, in which a hallucinatory procession of images challenges the protagonist to renounce his chastened character, stands as the metonymic master trope and driving desire behind the project that bears its namesake.

Among all the expected influences in Ritchie's own writing on the subject of diagrams, there were a few I did not expect to find. I was curious to see the reference to Edgar Allan Poe's protoscience fiction story, "A Descent into the Maelström," the tale of a ship that slips over the brink of a fantastic, all-consuming whirlpool in the North Sea, chronicled by an elderly Norwegian seafarer who remains its only surviving member who escapes by clinging to a wooden cask bobbing in the jet-black vorticular wall of water and rides the current back to the tranquil surface of the sea. For Ritchie, the relevance of the story is not only as another allegory of temptation and descent into the will of knowledge, but also as an inaugural work of "weird" or "speculative" realism (borrowing from H. P. Lovecraft and Ray Brassier, respectively). The story is driven less by the tension between the naked truth or falsehood of the narrator's claim—science fact or science fiction—and more by how an exacting, rational, and evidentiary voice bleeds into the irrational and the fantastic. The maelstrom is the place where the empirical and the journalistic intermingle with the irrational, the implausible, and this pushes the story beyond the binary of truth and falsehood. This calls for a logic of interpretation that displaces correlation with that of speculation, and the story posits the maelstrom as an uncanny epistemological figure that enables the reader the means of crossing the dangerous threshold of the unknown and unfathomable, while still living to tell about it. Put in the context of diagrams, for Ritchie, the maelstrom stands analogous to the inherent function of diagrams irrespective of their type or purpose, because they promote a process of speculation that helps us traverse uncharted territory. Or in the artist's own words, "whether we are truly accessing higher orders of reality or simply fantasizing that we are (which is the central question underlying mathematical formalism as well as art) diagrams are where concepts connect to their consequences, where ideologies are inexorably networked to the specific concepts and compromises that undergird or undermine them." Unlike maps, which only enable us to travel to places already known and familiar, diagrams are intermediary devices built from what is known and familiar, then used as a means of traveling into places that are not. To use a diagram demands a leap of logic—or a leap from one kind of logic to another—it is the cask in the water, the vessel that delivers us from the void.

I opened by relaying Ritchie's first studio installation at the Getty back in 2012 as it happened, with the hope that this essay might provide a small insight into his method at the earliest stages of development and illuminate the unremarked process that led to the current version of the project. But it now occurs to me this choice resonates with "A Descent into the Maelström" in another way: the fact that Poe's story is not merely told, but retold, from the seafarer's mouth to the ear of an anonymous secondary figure who did not experience the fantastic descent firsthand. Add the voice of Poe *qua* author to this equation, and contact with the maelstrom is already thrice removed in a receding narrative *abyme* (not to mention the silent, untold story of the protagonist's fallen shipmates lost beyond the point of no return), like my own clumsy adumbration of Ritchie's use of the story as an allegory for the diagrammatic imagination. The point here is that the dissimulation of address does not delimit the veracity of the account through distance, but rather exponentially increases the speculative possibilities of where the story might take us. The temptation functions much in the same way, and you following me following Ritchie after his first vertical drop into its swirling vortex, a ship lost beyond the diagrammatic horizon, can only enhance the speculative futures of this project.

The Temptation of the Diagram is a unique statement in the theory, philosophy, and science of the diagram, and in the history of diagrammatic art. It rejects a prescriptive reading, refutes orthodoxy, and resists universals, while at the same time it situates the diagram within a rigorously ordered descriptive system that invites speculation on new territories of the real. With the advent of this publication, a more enduring but no less personal encounter with the ongoing project will finally make its debut as document, archive, resource guide, book, and artwork. But I must here stop short of imposing an additional interpretive layer on the present version of the work, which would only do a disservice to the unfettered experience of discovery and exploration best left for each to delve into on one's own. It is impossible to predict the nature and extent of its future contribution to diagrammatic thinking, since by its very definition such exists in anticipation of unknown circumstances; however, it is certain the refrain of Matthew Ritchie's initial descent into the diagram will live on in lasting and unanticipated ways as it becomes available to a wider public.

REFERENCE LIST

Deleuze, Gilles. 1988. *Foucault*. Minneapolis: University of Minnesota Press.
Elmer, Greg, and Matthew Tiessen. 2013. "Deleuze/Foucault: A Neoliberal Diagram." *Media Tropes eJournal* 4, no. 1. http://www.mediatropes.com/index.php/Mediatropes/issue/view/1500/showToc.
Flaubert, Gustave. 1976. *Bouvard and Pécuchet*. Translated by A. J. Krailsheimer. Harmondsworth: Penguin.
———. 2001. *The Temptation of Saint Anthony*. Translated by Lafcadio Hearn. New York: Modern Library.
Glasgow, Janice. 1995. *Diagrammatic Reasoning: Cognitive and Computational Perspectives*. Cambridge, MA: MIT Press.
Harman, Graham. 2010. *Towards Speculative Realism: Essays and Lectures*. Winchester, U.K.: Zero Books.
Hobbs, Robert, with a foreword by Judith Richards. 2003. *Mark Lombardi: Global Networks*. Exhibition catalogue. New York: Independent Curators International, New York.
Holmes, Brian. 2007. "Network Maps, Energy Diagrams." April 27. https://brianholmes.wordpress.com/2007/04/27/network-maps-energy-diagrams/.
On, Josh. 2004. *They Rule*. http://theyrule.net.
Poe, Edgar Allan. 1976. "A Descent into the Maelström." In *The Science Fiction of Edgar Allan Poe*, edited by Harold Beaver, 72–88. New York: Penguin.
Ritchie, Matthew. 2008. "The Universe Is Infinitely Suggestive." In *The Morning Line*, edited by Eva Ebersberger and Daniela Zyman. Vienna: Thyssen-Bornemisza Art Contemporary.
———. 2014a. *The Temptation of the Diagram*. 2 vols. Seattle: CreateSpace.
———. n.d. "Temptation of the Diagram."
Stjernfelt, Frederik. 2007. *Diagrammatology: An Investigation on the Borderlines of Phenomenology, Ontology, and Semiotics*. Dordrecht: Springer.
Vidler, Anthony. 2000. "Diagrams of Diagrams: Architectural Abstraction and Modern Representation." *Representations*, no. 72 (Fall): 1–20.

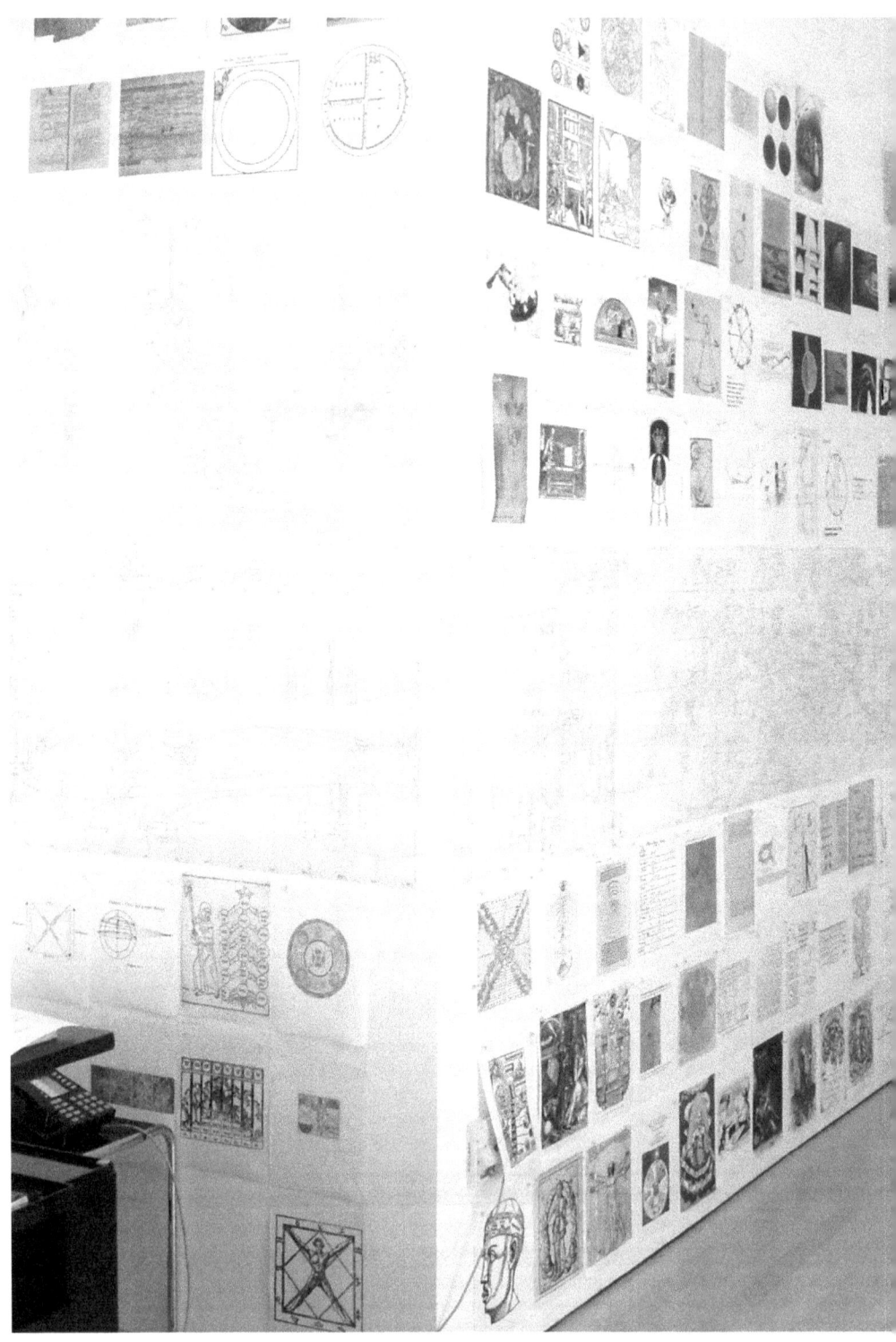

Matthew Ritchie, *The Temptation of the Diagram* in process at the Getty Research Institute, Los Angeles, May 2012.
Photo: Matthew Ritchie.

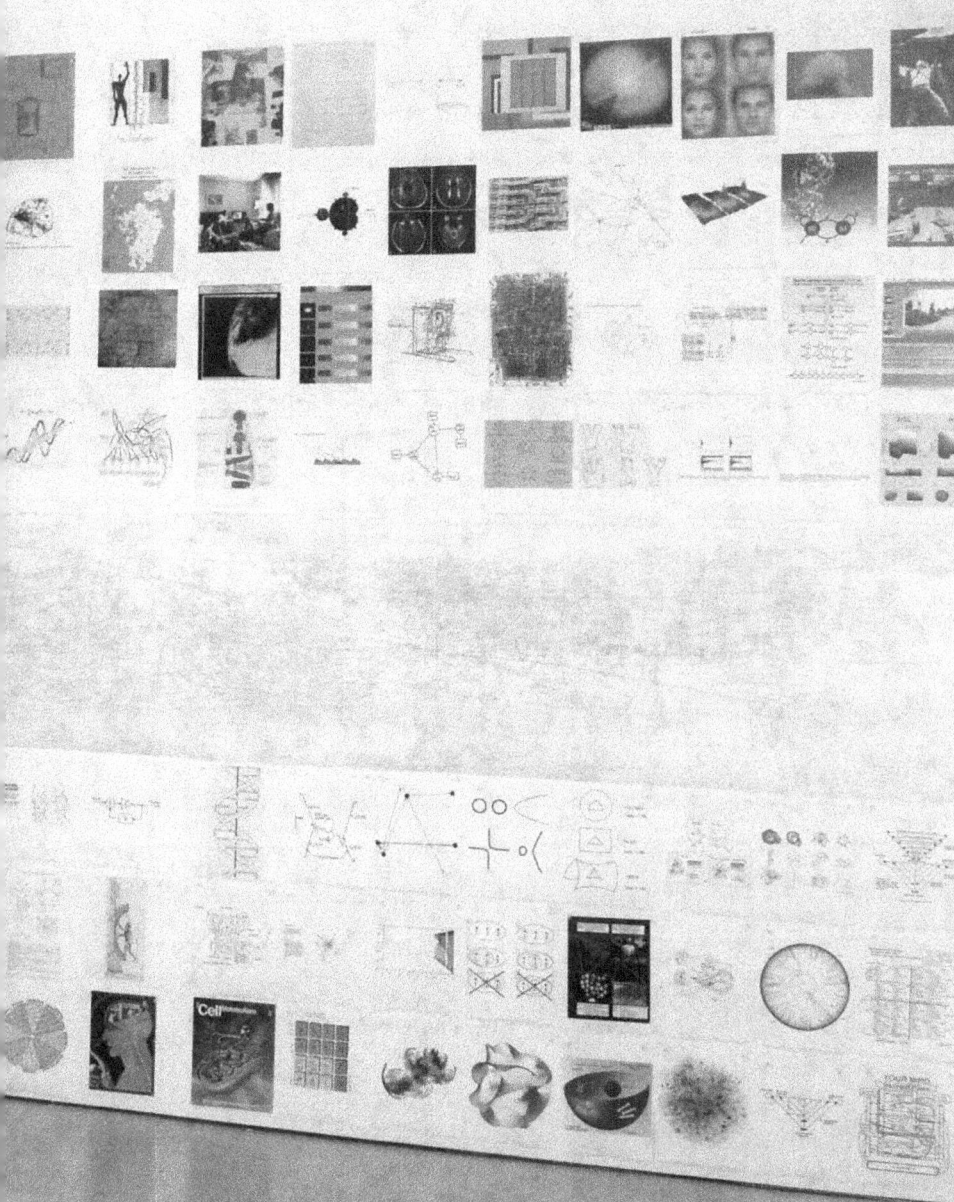

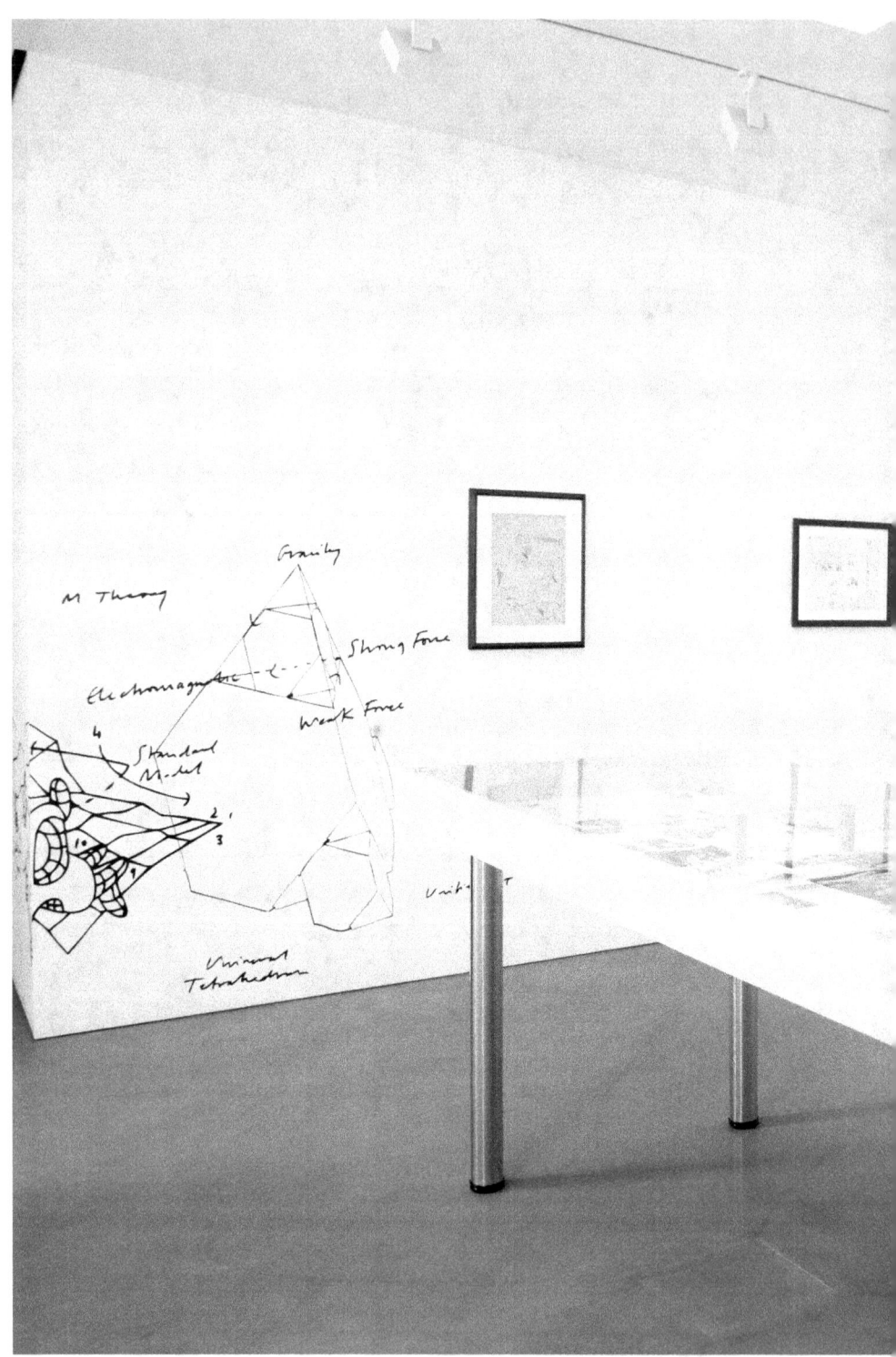

The Temptation of the Diagram (group form), Andrea Rosen Gallery, New York, March 30–April 27, 2013. The exhibition featured Aranda\Lasch, Archigram, Matthew Barney, Joseph Beuys, Earle Brown, Trisha Brown, Mel Bochner, John Bock, Lygia Clark, Max Ernst, Öyvind Fahlström, Thomas Hirschhorn, Steven Holl, Barry Le Va, Mark Lombardi, Thom Mayne, Julie Mehretu, Matt Mullican, Matthew Ritchie, Katy Schimert, Carolee Schneemann, Rudolf Steiner, Wolfgang Tillmans, and Bernar Venet. Organized by Matthew Ritchie. Photo: Jessica Eckert, Andrea Rosen Gallery.

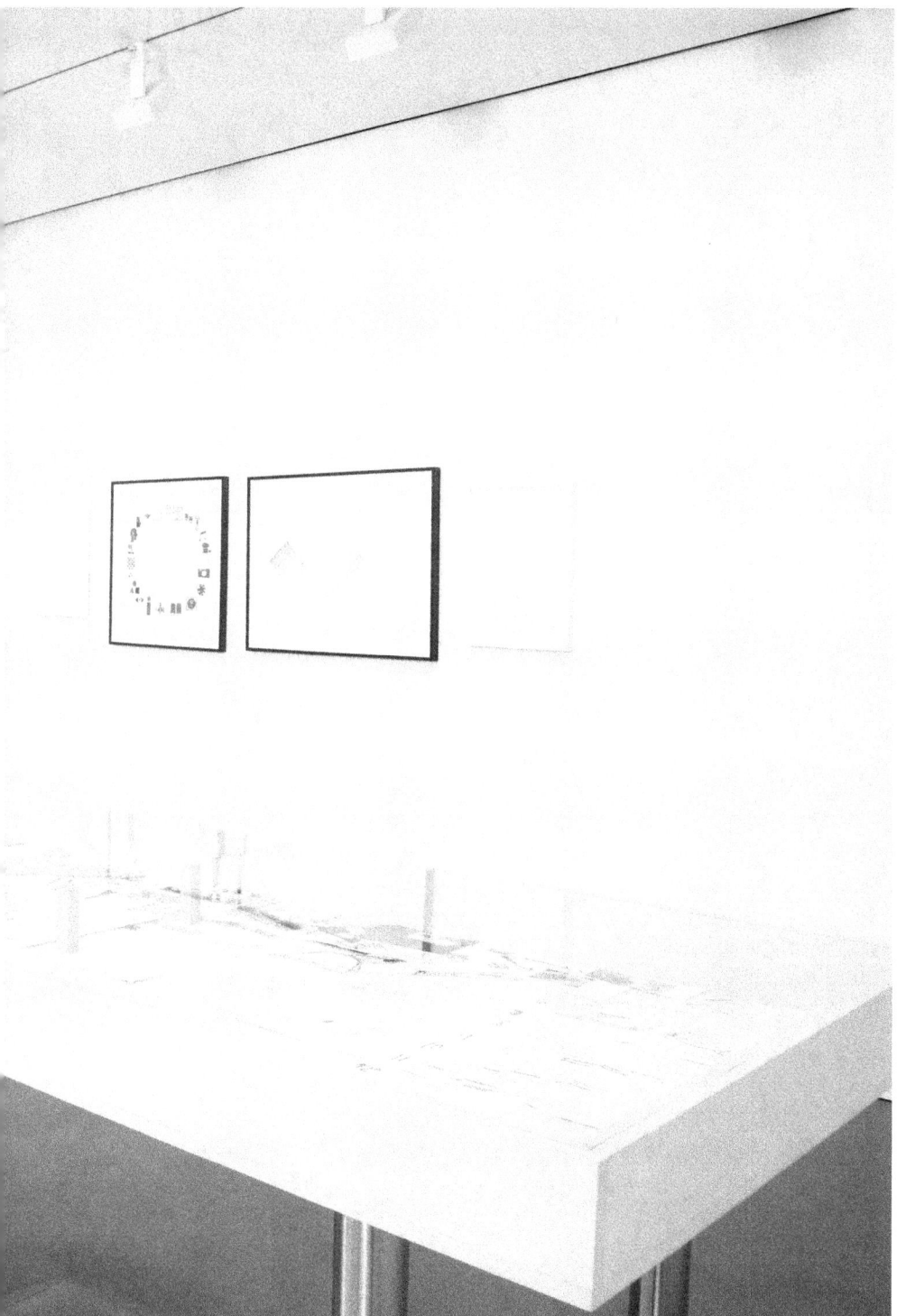

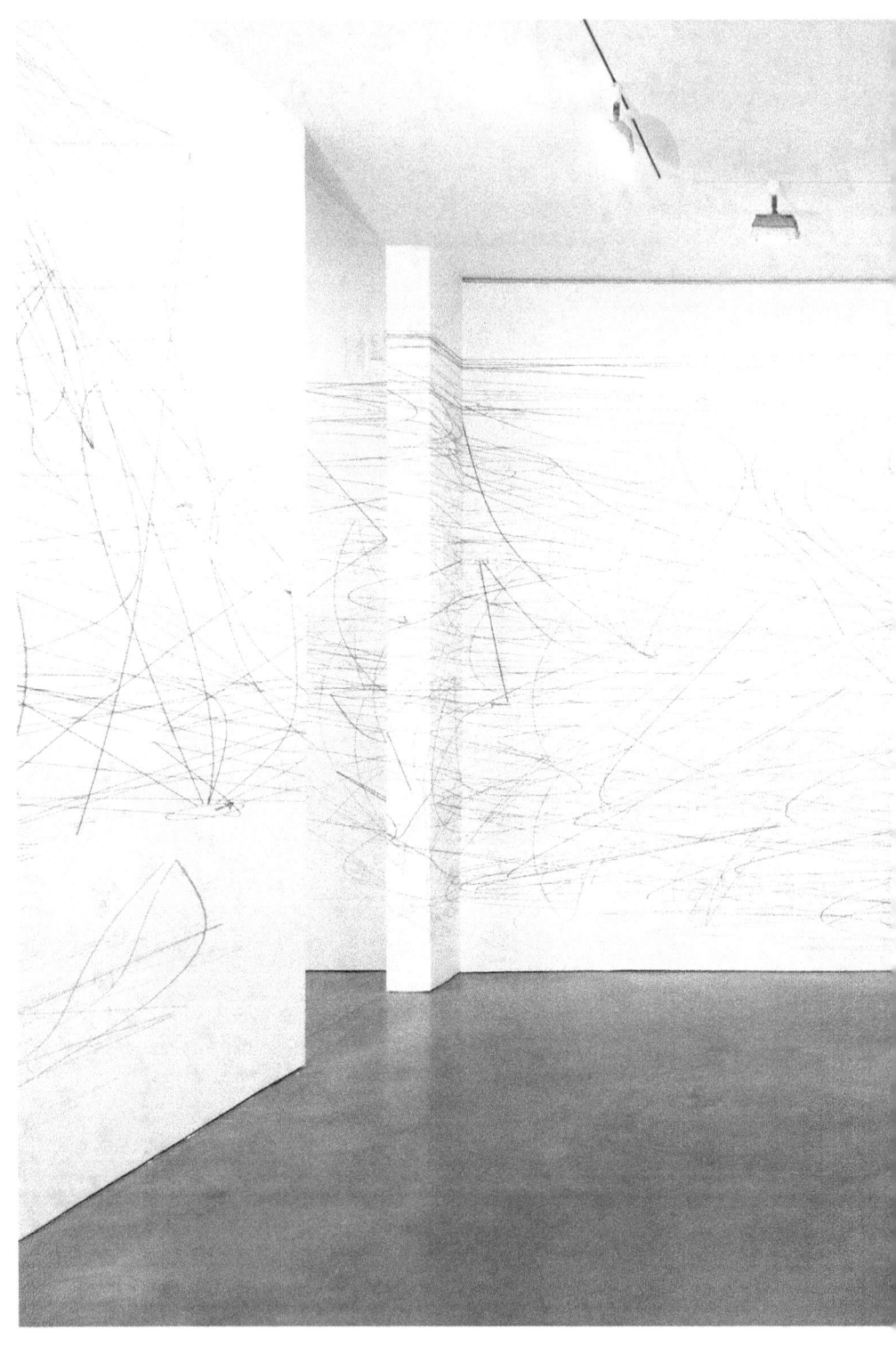

Matthew Ritchie, *The Temptation of the Diagram* (large form), installed as a part of *Ten Possible Links*, Andrea Rosen Gallery, New York, September 12–October 22, 2014. Photo: Lance Brewer, Andrea Rosen Gallery.

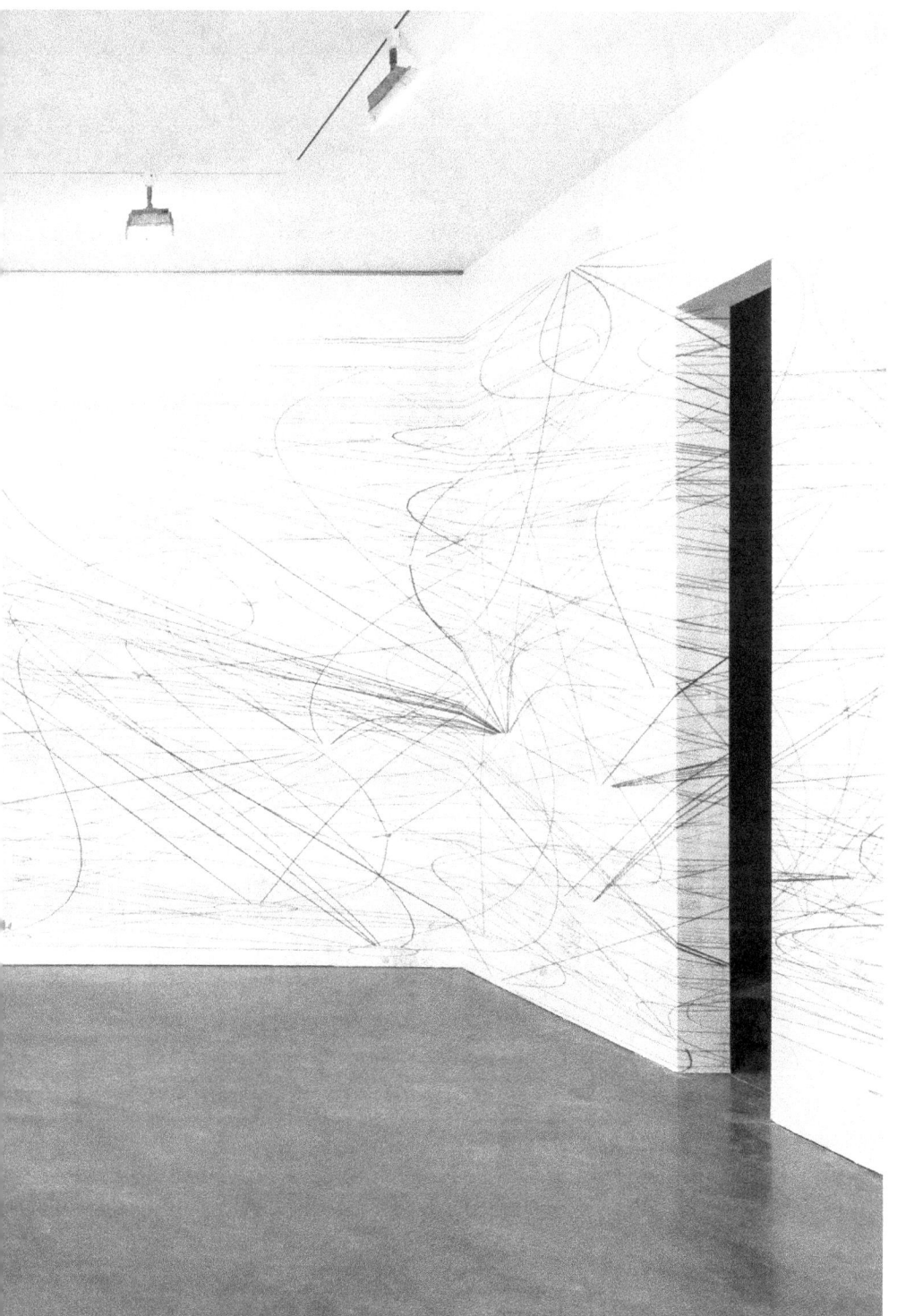

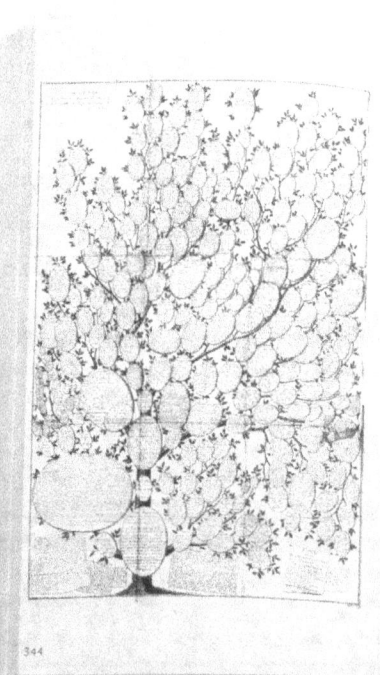

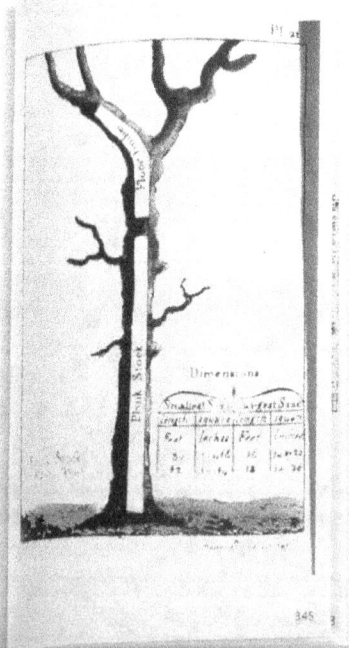

Matthew Ritchie, *The Temptation of the Diagram* (source book form). Photo: Pierre Le Hors, Andrea Rosen Gallery.

The Temptation of the Diagram
Matthew Ritchie

Book 2

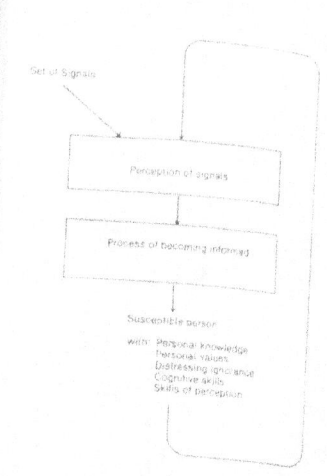

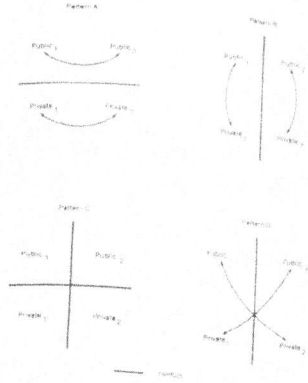

THE TEMPTATION OF THE DIAGRAM

MATTHEW RITCHIE

I

Somewhere there must be primordial figures whose bodily forms are only symbols. Could I but see them, I would know the link between matter and thought; I would know in what Being consists![1]
—Gustave Flaubert, *The Temptation of Saint Anthony*

In 2012, I was invited to attend the Getty Research Institute (GRI) for a scholar year with the research theme of "Artistic Practice." On theme, I spent my first week at the Getty as a solitary artist-in-residence, practicing staring out of the window at the Pacific Ocean, a view seemingly designed to induce either the kind of blankness perfectly conducive to deep and meaningful thought, or sleep. Upon my waking one day, the radical openness of the theme prompted me to reflect on a question about my own practice raised by Norman Bryson. "What is the primary material of my work?" I had always answered that question with two words, *information* and *drawing*, but now I wondered if I actually meant the kind of informational drawing we call diagrams.

By the second week, I was alert enough to search the Getty's index for books related to diagrams. Since it is primarily an art historical library, perhaps I should not have been surprised to find only a handful of entries. At an early point in my research I came across this quote by Susanne Leeb: "Diagrams escape the insoluble dialectic of absence and presence which pervades the play of representation, yet . . . diagrams have no status in art per se."[2] In art historical terms, the diagram is refuge and refugee, a universal visual bridge between the written and the seen, without a home in either. Artists' diagrams have long been regarded with suspicion, being sort of the janitorial staff of a drawing practice. But looking back at my own work before this project began, I could see that diagrams were a constant presence at every scale from architecture and performance scores to painting and drawing. In 2002, Patricia Falguières had even written about my work in precisely those terms saying, "what becomes meaningful here in the field of painting is the diagram itself as field of experience, as an intuitive practice."[3]

But diagrams are good at hiding in plain sight. With the help of the Getty staff and other scholars, it was gradually revealed that diagrams were present throughout the collection, almost omnipresent, and I quickly came to understand the term *diagram* is fugitive and constantly in flux, including not only artists' hand-drawn diagrams but also phase diagrams, maps, graphs, music and dance scores, cosmologies, fabrication drawings, patents, sketches, and circuit diagrams. The diagram is essential to wider applications such as large- and small-scale biological and physical network theory and the study of diagrammatic thinking, whose use in the selective processing of eidetic and physical choices is necessary to all theories of picture. To diagram is to intentionally compare and link alternatives, to indicate potential choices and boundaries, often establishing a conceptually clear boundary to indicate the limits of the comparison underway. A successful diagram not only expresses an underlying topology but also produces a manifold, or matrix, of terms where otherwise invisible force relations between pluralities of subjects can be articulated. Everywhere I have looked, from biography to biology, from warfare to epidemiology, from sociology to snowflakes, diagrams unpack the inscrutable mathematics of space, time, and energy and give them humanly accessible form. Diagrams, seen and hidden, constitute the pivotal means, or body, by which we can move through the overlapping topologies of prediction, memory, language, and metaphor without contradiction.

From that first simple question—what is the primary material of my work—I was drawn, once again, into the maelstrom of all human inquiry. This essay reflects the depth of that descent, fusing together all the related thoughts I have had working with specific aspects of diagrammatic thinking in art, science, and philosophy. Fused, it must be said, by someone who is neither a scientist nor a philosopher. Happily, the story of the diagram is populated by similarly independent eccentrics and category-eluding enthusiasts. The Temptation of the Diagram, the research project I commenced in 2012, became a multiyear effort that has included installations, books, and thematic exhibitions, culminating in a remarkable collaboration with the Getty Research Institute. During my residency, I explored the diagram in two ways, first by collecting and pinning up printouts of diagrams over the walls of the Getty studio[4] and, second, through a sectional drawing that gradually expanded to the exact size of the studio, matching human history to the limits of my practice. Although organized loosely as a time line of the use of diagrams across history, the project was always primarily concerned with relating the diagram as a tool of inquiry to both its expressive and causal forms. It is not a history of the diagram, but an art historical thought experiment, an anti-history, as the idea of the diagram itself constantly fights against the idea of linear development, preferring to proliferate in every direction, including across time. Like a tarot reading, or a "drunkard's walk," the diagrams selected from the edition and referred to in this essay constitute only one possible way to read the entire sequence.

The fully unfolded edition is a twenty-five-and-a-half-foot-long paper leporello, a type of accordion fold named for a character in Mozart's *Don Giovanni*, an opera that blends comedy, melodrama, and supernatural elements—much like this project. In this well-known story, the Don has seduced so many women that when his servant Leporello produces an account of his amorous activities, it comically unfolds into a ludicrously long document. This seems fitting. Although I have done my best to cloak this inquiry in scholarship befitting its origins on the Olympian heights of the Getty, it is at heart an extended love letter to a polyamorous muse. This edition's length is determined by the size of that original drawing, which itself is an index of the walls of the Getty studio. In its original installation, the collected source material was installed above and below the time-line drawing. For the edition, the drawing has been remade as an overlay that links 816 specific historical diagrams. This is far more than I originally placed on the walls of the Getty studio, but far fewer than the thousands I looked at. Already I have failed to equal the Don.

If it is becoming possible again to see painting as "a kind of quasi-person," as Isabelle Graw described it,[5] with drawing as its quasi-skeleton, then the diagram is its quasi-nervous system, the foundational connection between its parts and its precedents. Perhaps that is why we prefer the diagram hidden: it reminds us of the exposed nerves lying just below the skin. Maybe understanding this impulse can somewhat counter the residual presumption that thinking runs counter to aesthetic contemplation, that information is not beautiful. Flaubert once declared that God had made three perfect things, *Don Giovanni*, *Hamlet*, and the sea. The tortured hermit he imagined in *The Temptation of Saint Anthony* is besieged by an encyclopedic parade of gorgeous visions, yearning for a sustaining vessel in an ocean of meaning, hoping to reconcile the confusion that his other iconic creations, Bouvard and Pécuchet, would discover between signs, symbols, and reality in *The Dictionary of Received Ideas*. The diagram hovers between these states of enlightenment and confusion, the last, impossible temptation, an endless labyrinthine trace of our collective efforts to articulate and negotiate that almost impossible circumstance, reality itself.

II

The viewer will quickly notice that modern diagrams are freely and ahistorically interpolated throughout this project, starting with anthropological studies and genetic and language maps, including contemporary information that is specific to each location in time. For me, Geoffrey Sampson's essential diagram defines the first critical split in writing systems, between glottographic, or linear communication, such as speech and writing, and semasiographic, or picture-based, communication, such as diagrams (fig. 1).[6]

From their very first appearance, three of the most essential properties of the diagram are obvious; some kind of surface, the ostensible content, sometimes encoded in a notation system, and an implied or expressed connective line. But diagrammatic content cannot be divorced from diagrammatic form. The connective line is also a form of content, defining physical and metaphysical variation and positionality across time and space. Whatever the logical or symbolic notational languages used within the diagram, the subjects, or objects, of the diagram can be represented in timeless and spatially unbounded infinities or occurring across specific times and spaces.

The first diagrams were likely petroglyphs, carved in an inexplicably uniform style on every continent. These earliest connective drawings were the primary symbolic visual language of early humans for at least 20,000 years, communicating astronomical data and geographical information across and into vast swaths of cosmological time.

Although Sampson's diagram may seem to indicate a truncated evolutionary line, for such semasiographic systems as glottographic writing systems began to emerge, that is far from the case. Most early writing systems are inventories of repurposed and frozen diagrams. "How many?" and, "this way, or that?" they ask, with their indented triangles,

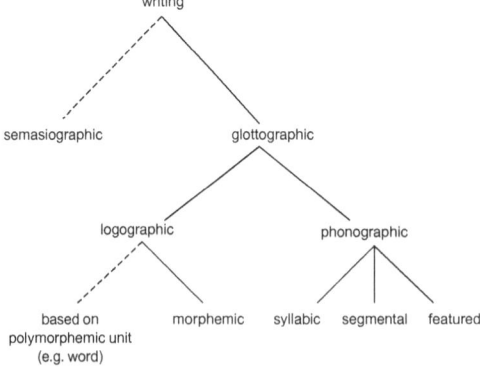

Fig. 1. Sampson divides writing systems between diagrammatic (semasiographic) and linear (glottographic) writing systems.

horned circles, stacked chevrons, and fletched arrows. In the pictographs, ideograms, and more abstract phonograms that begin to appear around 10,000 BCE, we can notice a notable change in surface function, as lighter, temporary, grounds slowly become the plane of immanence, what Paul Klee would one day call the "all-too-present white." The vast number of exquisite cosmologies, star maps, and divinatory games of chance that were chiseled into stone, baked into clay tablets, tattooed onto skins, and carved into bones by early civilizations make it clear that integrating space and time with the possibility of radical contingency—or to put it another way, exploring and narrating the possible range of predestination and free will, was always an urgent cultural requirement. Knowing where and when we are, the true nature of limits, and how meaning proliferates within and beyond those limits, is central to the story of the diagram.

As the inductive space of the magi was replaced by the deductive space of the philosophers, the gigantic system of Hellenistic thought coalesced out of this primordial soup of competing systems. Dominated by the luminous moons of Geometry and Logic, the question of what is "real" and what is "unreal" or "ideal" appears, along with the word "diagram." Diagrams like Euclid's postulates were understood as metonyms for mathematical propositions and hence nature itself,[7] offering an understanding of the hidden relations that might elude us when reading a written explanation of an idea. The promise of clarity, even certainty, in the geometry of the circle, the triangle, and the square is so perfectly suited to our lived experience that these essential diagrams both stimulate and constrain human thinking even today. At the same time, Euclidian geometry exemplified the idea that concepts can be both real and unreal at the same time. A geometric "point" has position, but no dimensions. As this purified form emerges in clear relief against its historical background, the inherent complexity of what constitutes a diagram becomes more visible. In what ways is an astronomical system, a map, or a game still diagrammatic? Is it in the same way a mathematical proof can be seen as a diagram?

First among equals in a long historical sequence of binary diagrams, Aristotle's description of term logic, expressed in the well-known "square of opposition," visually embodies the concept of limits (fig. 2). This diagram divides the world into things that are true and false. Anything, even the universe, can quickly be divided into opposed elements; such as good and evil but articulating such simple dichotomies also encourages the division of all reality into a series of axiomatic spaces or statements like fire, earth, water, and air. Aristotle's exclusionary diagram was one of discontinuous spaces, logically and physically separate. While the efficiency of the binary layout made it one of the most consequential and persuasive diagrams ever produced, the effort to somehow universalize its discontinuous terms led to centuries of scholastic and rationalist

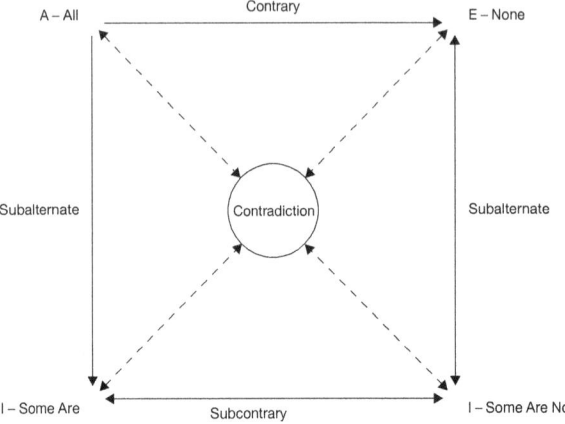

Fig. 2. Aristotle's square of contradictions, the most consequential diagram produced for a thousand years.

insistence on logically puzzling states of being such as sub-alternates and sub-contraries.

Inevitably, in such a pluralist and polytheistic society, exclusionary logic was not the only diagrammatic approach. In Figure 3,[8] Bruno Latour and Adam Lowe diagram the Hellenistic concept of copiousness where originality is the capacity to absorb an accumulation of causes and then produce a template sufficiently powerful that it will produce copies of itself. These copies will each contain the unique interrelational fecundity of the original composition, allowing us to both retrace the original causes and imagine new ones, quite different to the contemporary idea of the mechanical copy put forward by Walter Benjamin.

The Hellenistic link between description and diagram allows us to reconstruct the traces of a third and potentially unifying approach

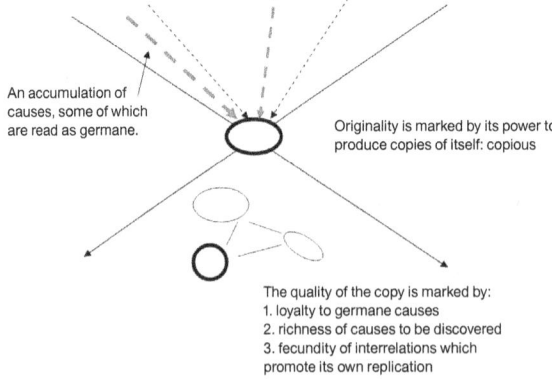

Fig. 3. The Hellenistic concept of copiousness.

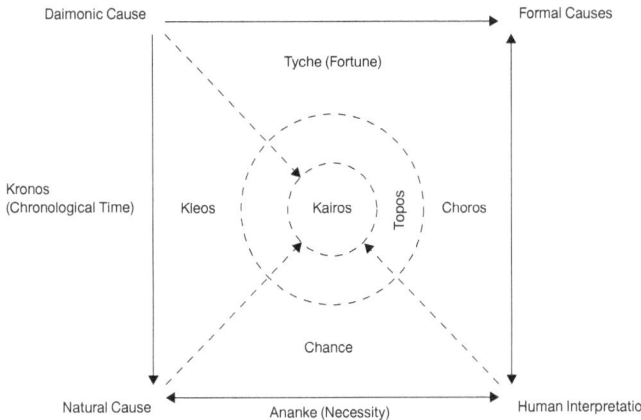

Fig. 4. Aristotle's logic of time combines *Ananke* (necessity), with *Kronos* (time), to produce *Kairos*: not just now, the *right* now. Similarly, the right place, or *Topos*, is more significant than *Choros*, the abstract set of all places.

that is essential to this project. In *On Interpretation*, Aristotle discusses future contingents by looking at the possibility of a sea battle.[9] Aristotle is interested in identifying the logic of a future that cannot be described by either the organic proliferation of options, or the square of opposition, an intermediate or "middle" space. In this example, there is no way to determine the true possibility of a sea battle the following day, only its relative probability. When the subject is an individual event occurring in the future, logical contradictions are meaningless, as such an event might just as easily not happen as happen.

Figure 4 presents Aristotle's intermodal logic inside a fourfold format that would prove as enduring as the square of opposition. The framing diagram shows four primary influences at the four corners; daimonic influences (daimons being a general term for the entities that embodied the distributive powers of destiny, including gods), natural causes, formal causes, and human interpretations, manifested in the form of *Tyche* or Fortune, a specific property in Hellenistic terms. The horizontal and vertical axes contrast the paired Hellenistic temporal concepts of *Ananke* (necessity), with the transdimensional *Kronos* of the earlier cosmic diagram (chronology). As the paired concepts interact, natural chance combines with *Tyche* to produce *Kairos*: not just now, but the *right* now, whose temporal result is *Kleos* or future correctness. Similarly, arriving in the right place, or *Topos*, is more significant than mapping *Choros*, the abstract set of all places. A hero, in these terms, is a vector that has found the only solution to the merciless contingencies of time and space. The Hellenes may have even invented the first analog computer, the Antikythera mechanism, to help predict fortuitous astronomical conditions and locations for such events.

III

Like all ideas, the culture of diagram has historical periods when it becomes either more or less distinct from the dominant visual language of its time. Early on, a potential limitation of diagrams seems to emerge. When new topologies or qualities are extended or added, others are often withdrawn or removed. The causal spatiality and metamorphic time of the Hellenic diagram did not survive its visual integration into Roman culture. The open diagram was absorbed into the functions of the state. Visual framing mechanisms stemming from the Aristotelian divisions and biblical genealogies became so ubiquitous that they were almost indistinguishable from policy, philosophy, medicine, mapmaking, and architecture, and it can be difficult to see such images as diagrams when they are so perfectly aesthetically integrated into documents, images, and structures. The Hellenic "daimon," an abstract figure of distributive destiny, became bound to the more literal and corrupted body of the Judeo-Christian "demon" and the interrelated concepts of *Tyche*, *Kairos*, and *Topos* were fused into a more rigid notion of "Fortune," specifically military success, that came to be identified with divine approval of moral behavior, an ossifying process paralleled in contemporary Hindi, Mayan, Buddhist, and Chinese philosophy. As the medieval empires developed complex diagrams of destiny and theories of fate bound to their ornate and circular chronologies, in Europe, *Ananke* and *Kairos* gave way to *Kronos* and *Kosmos* as the need to consistently endorse the messianic time foretold in the Bible relegated recognizably change-based diagrams, such as Nicolas of Oresme's graphs, to marginalia. Fortune, or Providence, was simply part of God's plan. Once a moral model of time was firmly embedded in the social construct and linked to a pre-specified "end of times," the central allegorical theme in medieval discussions of temporal logic became the conflict between the rival doctrines of divine foreknowledge and human freedom of action. The purpose of the serpent in the garden, the demon in the diagram, was consigned to myth.

But every effort to create an ultimate table of answers, to chase the demon from the diagram, produced even more questions. William of Ockham asked, "Can man be free if God already knows his fate?"[10] Muddling his way back to an intermodal logic, in his analysis of how time branches again and again, Ockham argued that although God must know the result of all future contingents, "the true future," human beings can still freely choose between the possibilities, a state that Juan de Molina called "Middle Knowledge." In Figure 5, this idea of the tree of time and the "true future" is indicated diagrammatically.

The free agent must operate in a continuous space and time to be free at all. This ongoing concern with relative freedom of movement or choice had significant ramifications for diagrammatic thinking. As

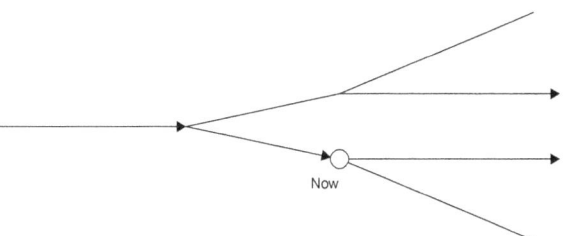

Fig. 5. A representation of branching time. The idea of the "true" future is indicated by the use of arrows showing the selected or "true" events.

Samuel Edgerton observes, "Strangely enough, it was this compression of body and space which paved the way for the eventual 'systemic space' of the Renaissance."[11] After the Roman state collapsed, the medieval theory of picture had become ever more discontinuous, pattern and image embedded but separated in Aristotle's carefully partitioned universe. By 1277, the contradictions of Aristotle's metaphysics had become so theologically complex it was forbidden even to teach them. The possibility of denunciation for demonic possession by articulating any deviation from orthodoxy meant the slow reemergence of the open diagram was necessarily conducted through a secretive and glorious collection of metaphors, trees of knowledge, alchemical emblems, cryptograms, astronomical notations, anatomical drawings, proposals for unique inventions, protoperspectives, and grotesqueries that characterize the many and curious protoscientific visual languages of the period. Edgerton cites Ernst Cassirer's list of four symbolic forms, language for verbal concepts, art for visual concepts, science for mathematical concepts, and myth for unexplainable natural phenomena, as the components of this language, arguing that "the human mind systematizes these symbols into structures that develop quite independently of whatever order might exist in the natural world."[12] Many of the diagrams I first came across in the GRI's collection exemplify this special moment in the evolution of scientific visualization, forming one of the many chains of images and forcing connections that can be found in *The Temptation of the Diagram*.

Given what we now know of space-time and relativity, where our future is already in the past of another light cone, the question of whether the position of any "true" future is knowable and what it means to change a given sequence of events in space and time is complex and is still very much a debate within both philosophy and the physical sciences. Nuel Belnap argues: "There is no real choice without the reality of alternative possible choices facing the agent, none of these possibilities is a ghostly image of some specially distinguished one among them that some philosopher might label "the actual choice."[13]

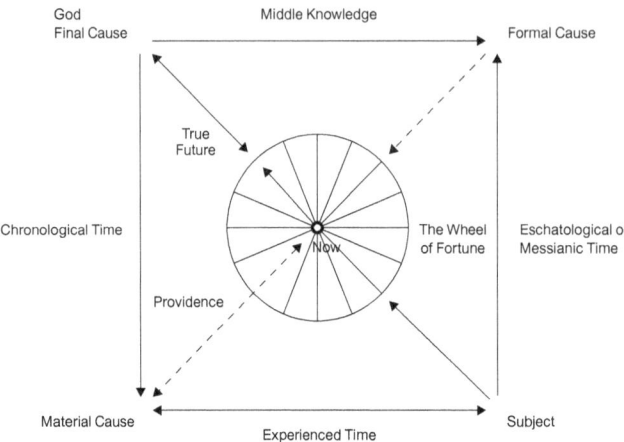

Fig. 6. The medieval concept of time requires three axes. Our lived experience, including the concept of free will, is conducted along one axis, while the eschatological process of messianic time unfolds along the other, paralleled by the axis of chronological or fixed time.

Once visualized as a diagram, this question shows we cannot ignore our own experience of linear, tensed or "experienced" time, or the physical reality of block, "chronological," deterministic time, or the human need for a moral, eschatological, or "messianic" sense of time that accounts for our own subjective projections.

The wheel of fortune, uncoupled from the state, became a way to represent the ambiguity of this triple space, simultaneously predestined and contingent. The medieval diagram reached its apogee Ramon Llull's *Ars Magna*. Dreaming of a universal theosophy, Llull devised a sort of paper computer, a cross between the Antikythera mechanism and a theological roulette wheel that could answer any question put to it—as long as it fell within Llull's ideas of universal concerns. In Figure 7, the wheel-like space of Llull's circular *Ars Magna* diagram, held by the figure on the left, can be seen guiding us to a protoperspectival staircase.

The combination of optical perspective and the printing press in Europe produced a newly liberated communicative space capable of integrating empirical and Christian models of continuity. Playing cards and biblical texts were the most widespread products of early printing, signaling an equal interest in games of chance and the rigid orthodoxies of the church, while linear perspective provided a diagrammatic form for divine grace to be unified with Euclidian geometry. Leapfrogging across civilizations and cultures in Europe, India, and Arabia, it is the gradual cross-pollination of these separate diagrammatic languages that links the mystical language of medieval diagrams with the systemic spaces of the Renaissance, taking us from the nested interiority of Dante's cosmos to the vast, post-Galilean universe of Milton. The transformative image

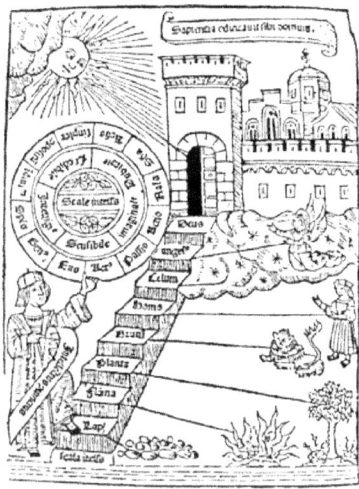

Fig. 7. In Ramon Llull's stair of intellect, the compartmentalized wheel of medieval space can be seen giving way to the systemic space of the Renaissance.

of the wheel of fortune reappears in Dante and Petrarch's "Triumphs," transforming into the compass rose that so embodied the segmented topology of luck central to the early modern conceit of a mercantile world, expressed most horribly in the triangular diagram of the slave trade. In the diagram of world systems theory proposed by Fernand Braudel and Giovanni Arrighi and shown in Figure 8, it is in the fifteenth century, that the idea of "transhumance"—a shared economic, climatic, migratory, and intergenerational experience, begins in a series of overlapping events and territories.

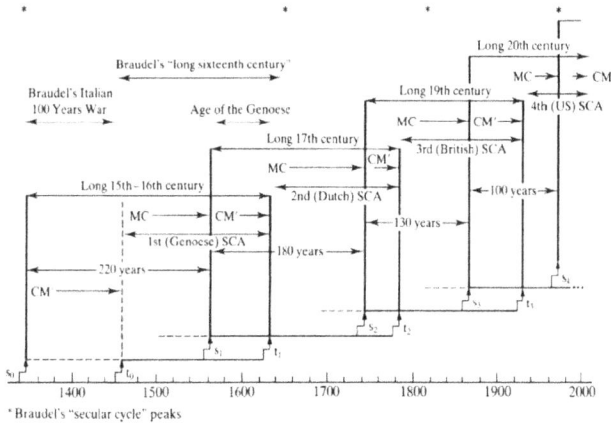

Fig. 8. Braudel's long cycles, extrapolated by Arrighi, propose that overlapping time-based experiences constitute our true culture.

IV

For John Bender and Michael Marrinan, the revival of the open form of the diagram in the seventeenth and eighteenth centuries is the foundation of what Krzysztof Pomian calls the "elements of discourse" in modern science[14]: the propositions, images, and theories that allow us to connect objects, forces, and interactions that would normally be inaccessible to us. For a century or two, the scientific diagram reacquired the glorious certainty that it was metonymical with reality itself.

In an age of extraordinary diagrams, Isaac Newton's optical theory from his *Opticks* of 1730 and his diagram of gravitational relations were perhaps the most scientifically consequential examples (figs. 9, 10), although the foundational works of René Descartes, Robert Hooke, and Gottfried Leibniz (and so many, many others) were also expressed in extraordinary diagrams and lay equal claim to our attention. After uniting physics and geometry though diagrams in his *Opticks*, Newton inverted the Hellenic relation of *Topos* and *Choros*, arguing that an ideal or abstract space defines the production of all places across the universe.

For all their idealism, the efforts of such open diagrams to cut across scientific boundaries were still bound to the rules of exchange that governed access to the disciplinary arrays that Michel Foucault describes in his diagram of the seventeenth- and eighteenth-century empirical spheres in *The Order of Things* (fig. 11).[15] For more than a thousand years, Euclid's fifth postulate had entangled theories of geometry with the idea of synthetic a priori knowledge, a belief that our knowledge of space was a truth that we were born with. As mechanical clocks and voyages of exploration filled in the empty parts of space and time, an ever more comprehensive and definitive social model, where each individual occupied a relative "position" in "the system of the world," took hold.

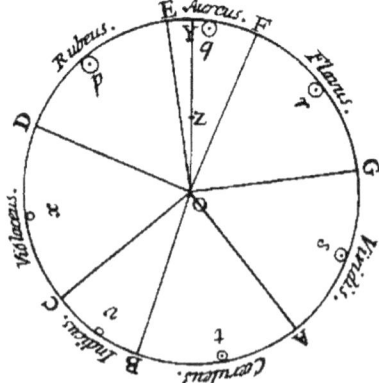

Fig. 9. Isaac Newton united physics and geometry in his *Opticks*.

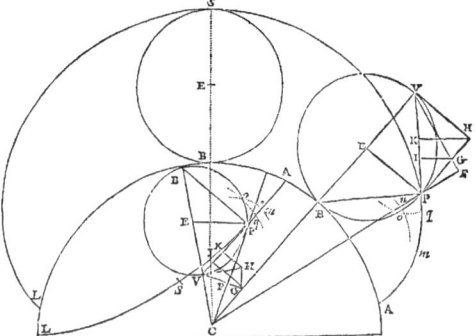

Fig. 10. Isaac Newton's diagram of gravitational relations, uniting *Choros* and *Topos*.

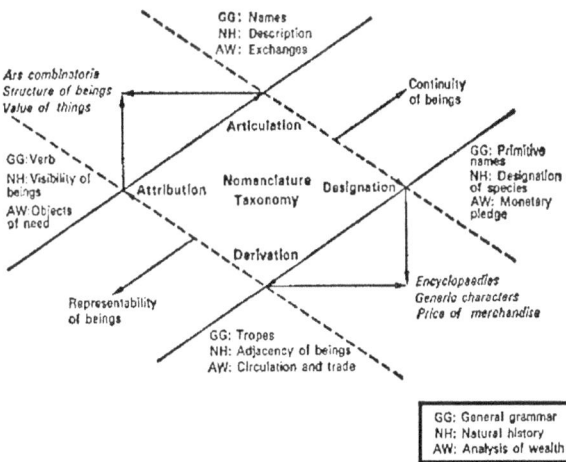

Fig. 11. Michel Foucault diagrammed the disciplinary arrays of the seventeenth and eighteenth centuries.

With a rational universe to play in, perhaps the rules of the human project could become the index of the diagram. The global enthusiasm for empiricism and empire resulted in ever more heroic and absurd efforts to classify, list, chart, and graph every aspect of Newton's purportedly unitary space, fueling the fantasy of a rational and ever more comprehensible universe, an infinite diagram. By 1726, they would be so ubiquitous that Alexander Pope would refer to them dismissively as "the minute wire drawings of scholastic investigation,"[16] a proliferation perhaps most comprehensively and beautifully illustrated by Thomas Malton's *A Compleat Treatise on Perspective in Theory and Practice* from 1775 (fig. 12).

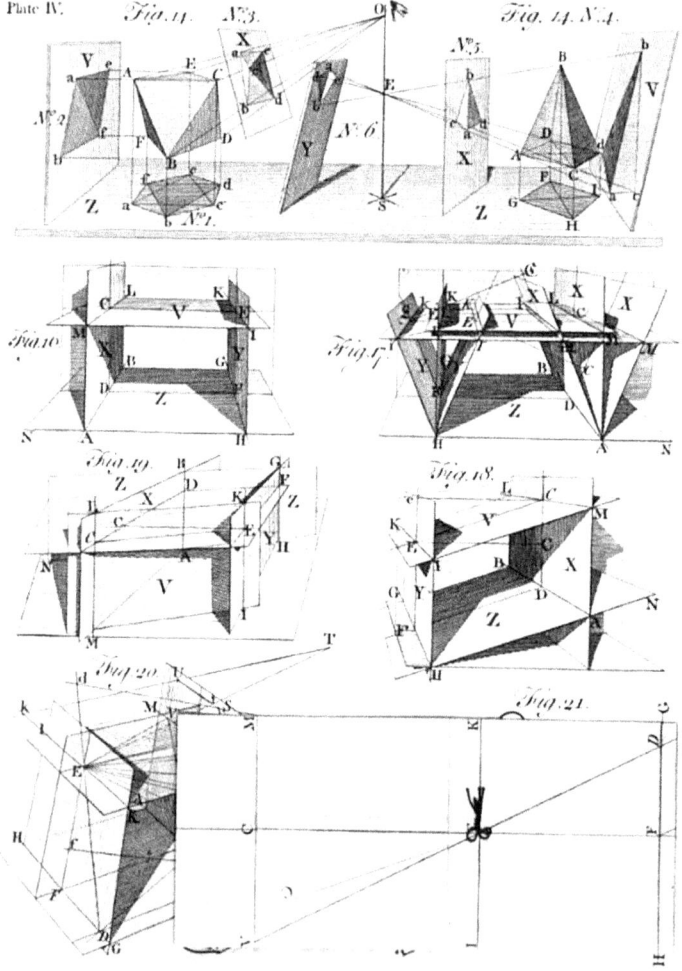

Fig. 12. Thomas Malton explored Euclidian perspective to the ultimate extent.

In his introduction to *The Order of Things*, Foucault cites Jorge Luis Borges's fictitious "Celestial Emporium of Benevolent Knowledge" to illustrate the arbitrariness of any such effort to categorize the world. Ironically, Borges's imaginary book was based on one of the real ancestors of our own dictionaries and encyclopedias, John Wilkins's *An Essay towards a Real Character and a Philosophical Language* (1668) which had proposed a universal philosophical language. By 1726, Jonathan Swift was already satirically describing "The Engine" in *Gulliver's Travels*, a protocomputer directly descended from Llull's *Ars Magna* that could automatically "write" nonsensical books on the arts and sciences, while at the same time, from Wilkins's poetic roots would grow John Harris's *Lexicon Technicum* (1704), Ephraim Chambers's *Cyclopedia* (1728), and Denis Diderot's *Encyclopédie* (1751). For Immanuel Kant, thought was predicated on a logical architecture, the "schema," a diagram whose production he called "the hidden art" (fig. 13). Although the schema was based on a distinction between form and content, or phenomena and noumena, it was also an image in process, a diagram. How the schema moved between empirical intuition and sensible understanding remained mysterious. In the fashion of Aristotle, the categories of the schema remain mystically distinct, and while Kant used a compartmentalized system to describe it, he never quite articulated the possibility that the "hidden art" might be the diagram itself.

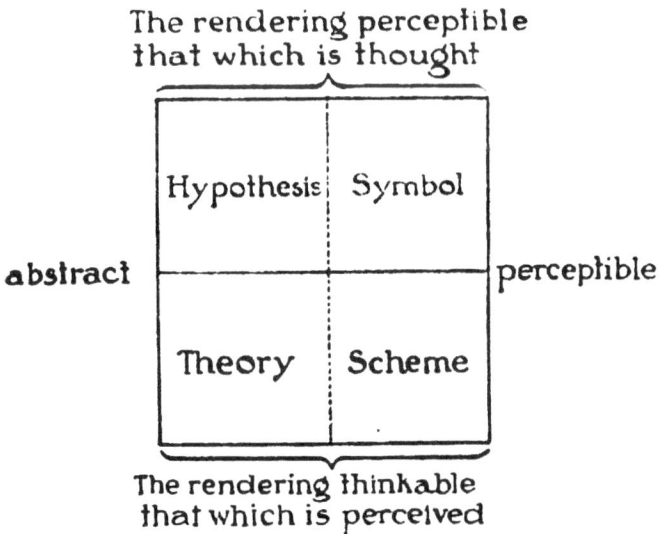

Fig. 13. How the schema moved from pure reason to the objective world via sensible understanding remained mysterious.

V

The exploration and resolution of this dilemma would be the basis for the next metamorphosis of the diagram. In the early nineteenth century, when the "sacred geometry" of Euclid and Newton's classical mechanics encountered the newly discovered laws of thermodynamics and the emergence of probability theory, the paradoxes of Euclidian geometry and the limits of two dimensional metonymical diagrams were exposed. In the early twentieth century, they would be confounded.

The mysterious "leaping dance" of atomic motion hypothesized by Democritus had been brought back into contemporary focus by Robert Brown's observations of Brownian motion and elevated to the status of axiomatic scientific problem by Pierre Simon Laplace in 1814 when he proposed the first scientific articulation of determinism, proposing, "An intellect which at a certain moment would know all forces that set nature in motion, and all positions of all items of which nature is composed . . . embracing in a single formula the movements of the greatest bodies of the universe and those of the tiniest atom."[17] The medieval question of omnipotence and free will, once pondered by Ockham and Molina had been re-embodied in the form of an omnipresent "intellect."

Later thinkers would come to call Laplace's "intellect" a "demon" as it became clear it would violate the irreversible laws of thermodynamics. The idea of a demon in the diagram, a flawed master diagrammaticist, fascinated Laplace's contemporary, the spiritual vizier of the alternate, William Blake, in whose work we can find a literary and visual example of the struggle to identify the terms of this new and complex interaction between the human creative will and the need for new universal formal terms through which it can be expressed.

In the prose poem "Jerusalem," Blake's inner daemon, the fictional demiurge Los, proclaims, "I must Create a System, or be enslav'd by another Mans." To illustrate his system, Blake produced a hybrid Aristotlean-Venn diagram of his cosmology that neatly carves the Eternal Man into four parts; "for all things are fourfold, and repeat in miniature the great fourfold of the universe."[18] But although Blake built his universe around the kind of prototype Venn diagram first found in Ramon Llull's work, its content and connective intent are quite different.

Blake's diagram offers more than a simple rethinking of the relationship between idea and source (fig. 14). In the narrative, Blake has cast himself as a master game player, infinite, like Laplace's "intellect," but willing to rewrite reality and mythology to suit his narrative. Blake's diagram confronts the Newtonian "system of the world" with its own demon, an intermodal individual, an imaginative free agent willing and capable of incorporating multiple positions and perceptual categories. We recognize in Blake not only a passion for metaphor as the only suitable state of mind in a political climate where literal meanings have

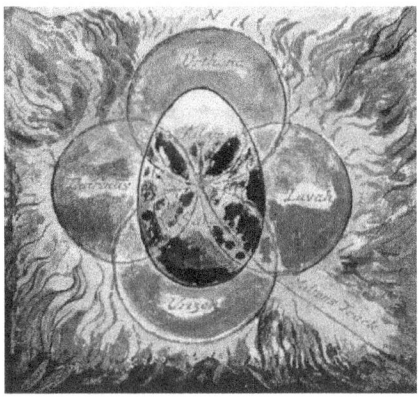

Fig. 14. Blake's diagrammatic cosmology is a bridge between the rigidly compartmentalized spaces of the medieval diagram and the shared spaces of set theory.

become impossibly compromised, but that he is the author of the first purely imaginative diagram. Reintegrating myth into language and art, Blake restores the symbolic function of the diagram—but now under the imaginative control of the author.

True Venn diagrams, among other mathematically axiomatic spaces, were essential to the later emergence of the revolutionary branch of logic called set theory, which emerged in the 1870s (fig. 15). The central paradox of set theory is that for any system or "set," like a world or a book or a diagram, there is always another set that includes it. In turn, this larger set is enclosed by an even larger one, and so on. Since it is almost impossible to deal with the implications of this, which require visualizing the large-scale general structure of the universe and

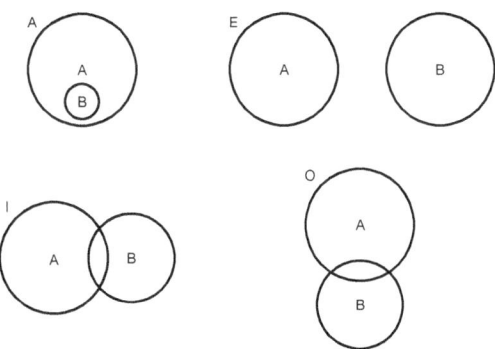

Fig. 15. John Venn's set diagrams, versions of which were proposed by Euler, Blake, Weber, and Llull.

the specific details of daily life in the same referential frame—this self-referential feedback often leads to either a repudiation of the closed world or a retreat to a kind of stupor when dealing with universal themes. The ideas themselves are consigned to the limbo that Slavoj Žižek calls the "Big Other." Blake, as a representative of a certain kind of artist, the kind of artist that is interested in diagrams, stands against this position. The diagrammatic property most strongly expressed through Blake's art is its ability to redeem the general and the specific simultaneously by creating worlds within worlds, amassing detail upon detail while understanding that the inevitable contradictions and oscillations that will violate the system (in a way that in physics could be called symmetry breaking) are essential to both its small-scale structure and its large-scale operation. Although it may seem paradoxical to think of a book or diagram deriving its integrity from being to some extent incomprehensible, the difficulty of reducing Blake's work to any of its elements remains one of his greatest strengths. Drowning in a sea of empirical facts and sensing the passing of an era in the West where unknown powers could be invoked to sustain moral choices, Blake made the claim that it was possible to assert a universal position through invention, setting the stage for a new kind of literature.

VI

The ways of God in Nature, as in Providence, are not as our ways; nor are the models that we frame any way commensurate to the vastness, profundity and unsearchableness of His works, which have a depth in them greater than the well of Democritus.

—Joseph Glanvill, as quoted by Edgar Allan Poe in his introduction to "A Descent into the Maelström" (1841) [19]

In Edgar Allan Poe's story, "A Descent into the Maelström," a fisherman recounts how he survived an enormous whirlpool, describing how he had coolly observed the various features of the terrifying gulf with an "unnatural curiosity," and then, following the principles of Archimedean physics, had lashed himself to a barrel, the only geometric form that can be successfully propelled out of the abyss. It is a story that is a description of a diagram.

Poe's story has been characterized as an early form of scientific fiction or science fiction (a term whose inverse complement might easily be the phrase *weird realism* coined by H. P. Lovecraft, of whom, more later). In his fiction, Poe always maintains a narrative rigor and personal distance, no matter how horrific or extreme the phenomena might be. In "The Philosophy of Composition" (1846), he wrote, "It is my design to render it manifest that no one point in a composition is referable either to accident or intuition—that the work proceeded, step by step, to its completion, with the precision and rigid consequence of a mathematical problem."[20] In this scrupulous juxtaposition of informational and imaginative spaces, we find a doubled premise, first, that the ways of God (or contingency) are "not as our ways," and second, that human cognition now needs metaphorical literary technologies to extend itself effectively into the transitional areas and new sensory experiences that were recently liberated from superstition by science. Like Mary Shelley, Poe saw nature and man as antagonists in a horror story quite sufficiently strange and sublime to generate its own demons—which we may yet find only partially comprehensible. He avoids describing explicitly symbolic, fantastical, or supernatural elements extending beyond human terms of reference. In his opus *Eureka, A Prose Poem* (1848),[21] Poe further advances the concept of a rational but divine universe, using a single evocative diagram (fig. 16).[22]

In universalizing the author-centric agenda of his diagram, Poe qualifies the symbolic order reintroduced by Blake and proposes that imagination is simply a form of logical thinking. Thought, meaning, and speech are isomorphic across an invariant structure.

Beginning in the 1860s, the American logician Charles S. Peirce would take this concept considerably further. For Peirce, logic was the formal semiotic that preceded all metaphysics. Like the work of Llull, Leibniz, and Swift, his work is sometimes cited as a precursor to the digital computer. Essentially diagrammatic in nature, it was an effort to identify the identity of the sign,[23] the visual precursor to all possible forms of understanding, even the imagination itself. Refining a triangular diagram that went back to Aristotle, Peirce identified three elements in any instance of signification: the sign or type, the object or signifiant,

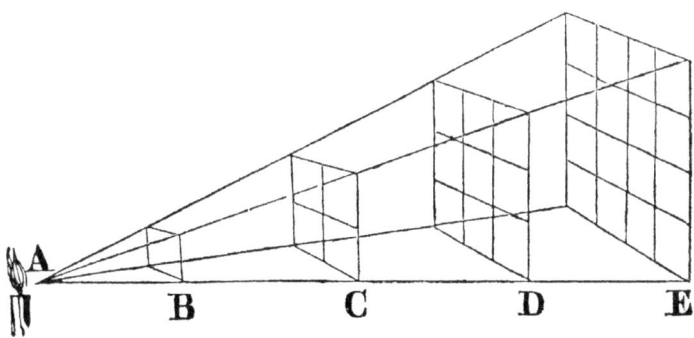

Fig. 16. Poe advanced the Euclidian concept of a divinely and diagrammatically rational universe, using a single evocative diagram in *Eureka, A Prose Poem*.

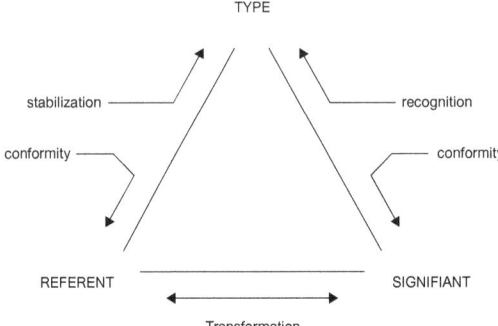

Fig. 17. C.S. Peirce's semiotic triangle.

and the referent, or us (fig. 17). A diagram contains all three. Iconic representations are the closest to what we usually think of as signs or pictures, having some of the immediate qualities of the signified, like a picture, or a recording. Symbolic conventions, like formal languages or abstract road signs, do not need to resemble the signified at all, but must be learned to have any meaning. The Index is the set of causal relations or intuitive signals that allows us to intuit the meanings of Icons and Symbols when they are not immediately visually apparent or formally deducible. A diagram is, of course, also the Symbol, Icon and Index of itself. Part of Peirce's early sign theory was that an infinite number of other signs could connect to any individual sign. Over many decades, the components of this system grew ever more complex, culminating in sixty-six classes of sign.

Peirce called the axis between the signifiant and the referent the axis of "transformation," or abduction, positing the relational imagination, or "fantasy," as work product of a rational system, and he stipulated both that chance and continuity (or as he called them, tychism and synechism) are fundamental properties of an evolving universe. For Charles Darwin, the similarly contingent and continuous actions of nature on the evolutionary selection of species could better shown through a branching tree diagram illustrating the connections between the vast diversity of forms catalogued in the previous centuries (fig. 18). For Darwin's cousin Francis Galton, the prospect of such genetic difference would lead to eugenics, and grotesque efforts to limit that proliferation.

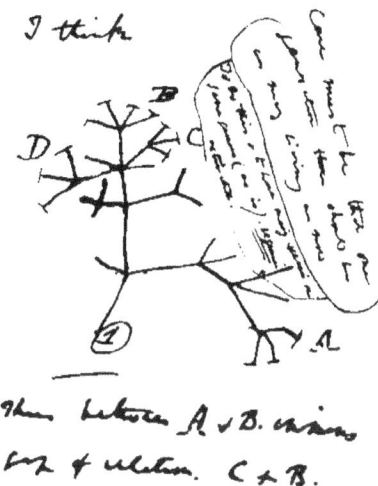

Fig. 18. For Charles Darwin, a simple tree diagram held the key to the proliferation of forms produced by natural selection.

In the era that would produce Sherlock Holmes, deductive minds everywhere sought similar narrative completion through projective ratiocination and the production of new cultural forms. The exploded geometric spaces of Gaspard Monge's technical drawings, Charles Hinton's images of categorical cubes, Edwin Abbott's *Flatland: A Romance of Many Dimensions* (1884), and Henri Bergson's cone of memory were all symptomatic of this overwhelmingly connective approach. Even the apparent randomness of reality could be diagrammed. Louis Bachelier's *Theory of Speculation* (1900) proposed the fluctuating value of stocks be used as the model for a stochastic modeling process that could as easily trace the path of a molecule, or the path of an insect or bird in flight. Patent applications for engines, automobiles, radio, telephones, kinematographs, aircraft, machine guns, and electrical transmissions show an obsession with acceleration, while newspapers, military maps, and sociological charts show a society dedicated to instrumentalizing new forms. As these new technologies integrated areas of time and space that had been isolated for millennia, social concepts and physical objects were forced into sudden juxtaposition. Exposure to these radical, often surreal, shifts in scale and speed, renewed interest in the universally communicative potential of symbolic languages and revived an interest in experimentation, or fantasy, as being another logical product of any large-scale inquiry into the diversity of the universe. In *Alice in Wonderland* (1865), Lewis Carroll used the metaphor of a pack of playing cards, a formal device that had become popularized as a divinatory diversion to explore the limits and rules of chance and language; while Stéphane Mallarmé's ludic poem "Un coup de dés jamais n'abolira le hasard" (1897) places another shipwreck survivor, consumed by a maelstrom of systems, chance, and myth, inside a game of words. As has recently been demonstrated by philosopher Quentin Meillassoux, the apparently scattered layout of the poem conceals a rigorous diagrammatic logic that conspires to "vectorize the subject with a meaning, with a direction freed from ancient eschatology."[24] When Mallarmé (like Flaubert, an admirer of Poe) writes that "the poetic act consists in suddenly seeing that an idea splits into a number of motives of equal value and in grouping them,"[25] he almost seems to be echoing Poe's "Philosophy of Composition," proceeding with the precision and rigid consequence of a mathematical problem.

In his magisterial *Diagrammatology*, Frederik Stjernfelt suggests a reconsideration of diagrammatic thinking that links Peirce's theory of semiotics, premised on the concept of thought, meaning, and speech being isomorphically connected across an invariant structure, such diagrams being coextensional with mathematics and theories of picture, to Edmund Husserl's analysis of representational forms and his series of time diagrams from the early twentieth century that added new properties to the diagram of time. In Husserl, the past is referred to as "a continuum of phrases" and the present as a "series of nows," perhaps filled with other objects, a sequence of positions in time, a possible diagram of the future.

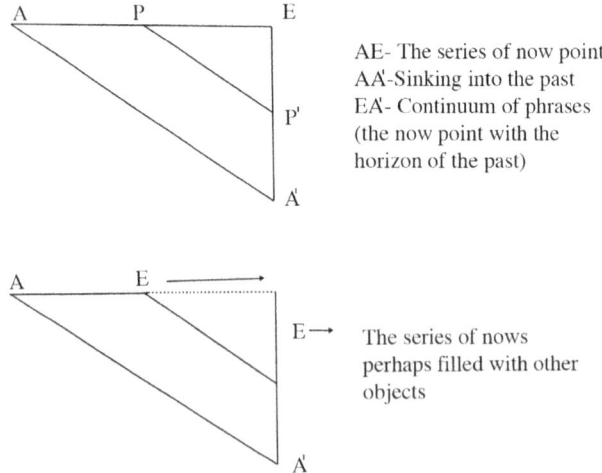

Fig. 19. Husserl's diagrams sought to integrate time with the phenomena of consciousness.

Husserl's diagrams sought to integrate time with the phenomena of consciousness but they remained unattached to space (fig. 19). Husserl contended that scientific realism takes "physical objects and their determinations [to be] correlatives of logical, categorical, theoretical thinking, and therefore not experienceable in sensory experience, which is misconstrued as being taken as implying unknowability." In contrast, for Husserl, "to posit a noema, or thought, is to posit the object corresponding to the noema. The object appears within the noema as the moment of unity among its constituent predicates."[26]

In other words, you know it as you see it. To juxtapose the elements of a diagram across time is to predicate the diagram's own existence as a moment of unity across time. Being an object of pure thought, the diagram, or fantasy, needs only its components to be named. Peirce and Poe had both hoped to identify the source of imagination in a logical diagram, solving the question of imagination through the philosophical equivalent of deriving optical perspective from Euclidean geometry. Husserl proposed that our experience of time must precede any logical space it might describe.

For Stjernfelt, a reconciliation between these positions is accomplished through the diagram itself. In building diagrams of thought, we are constructing a variable, incorporeal body for the eidetic exploration of the enormous variety of objects, spaces, and times that parallels our actual bodily experiences. Critically, the diagrammatic conventions used by Husserl and Peirce remained semasiographic and are not dependent on the conventional organization of meanings linked to human experience of time and space. They are juxtapositional, not positional in time and space. By the beginning of the twentieth century, developments in the physical sciences demonstrated the fullest extent and necessity of such imaginative vehicles.

VII

By the 1850s, Nikolai Lobachevsky, Carl Friedrich Gauss, and János Bolyai had theorized something impossible to imagine, a non-Euclidean spatial geometry mathematically deducible from Euclid's fifth postulate. The question as always, was how to integrate the fixed positions of space with the changing positions of time. Equations of state proved hard to visualize in non-Euclidian spaces. In 1873, Josiah Gibbs proposed using "certain diagrams of different construction...to arrive, for example, at the conception of energy, of entropy, of absolute temperature, in the construction of the diagram without the analytical definitions of these quantities."[27] Using only visual thinking, the relationship between energy, entropy, and volume was envisioned as a surface, creating a dimensional surface related to the new axes of energy, entropy, and volume. After carefully studying Gibbs's publications, in 1875 James Clerk Maxwell first drew and then sculpted Gibbs's surface, visualizing temperature curving over space and time in four dimensions (fig. 20). By mechanizing change, Maxwell's drawing systematizes Laplace's urge and asks a new question, how to best visually represent the invariant laws of physics under different transformations. Can we diagram our knowledge of time and space while we are still within it?

Unlike Laplace, Maxwell understood that energy, matter, and the information that defines them is constantly in flux. Working on the assumption that although matter may be irreversibly doomed to follow the arrow of time, an ideal intelligence may yet allow us to step outside

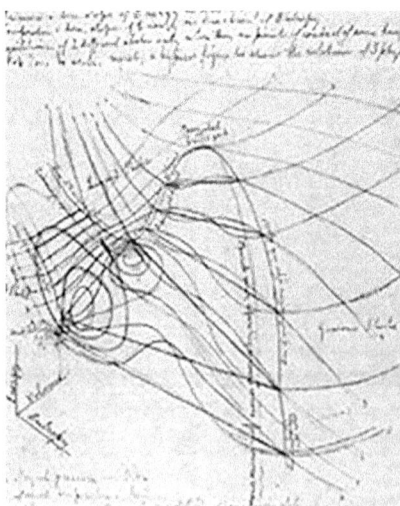

Fig. 20. James Clerk Maxwell's drawing of the thermodynamic surface introduced curvature across time.

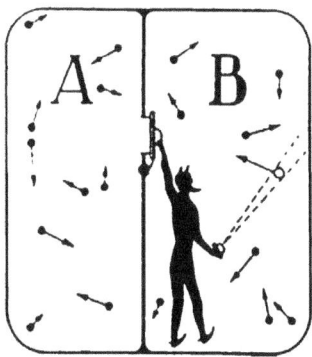

Fig. 21. Maxwell's Demon at work.

the process, he proposed a response to Laplace's demon, an entity of his own in the form of "a neat-fingered mathematical doorkeeper" (later dubbed a "sorting demon"). Maxwell's demon could step in and out of the diagram at will, changing the state of any physical system by using pure information to create energy. Perhaps there might be no proportionate energy cost for using information, permitting the creation of perpetual motion machines that could circumvent the second law of thermodynamics.

Maxwell's demon was only one of several stubborn questions of computation, randomness, and probability that had survived from the time of Aristotle. The diagrams generated by Maxwell and Henri Poincaré together with Lobachevsky's and Lorentz's non-Euclidian geometry had prepared the way for the geometrical model of space-time proposed by Albert Einstein and Hermann Minkowski in 1907, a four-dimensional space-time, terminating both the Euclidean concept of an unalterable form of space and Husserl's inquiries into an independent form of time (fig. 22).

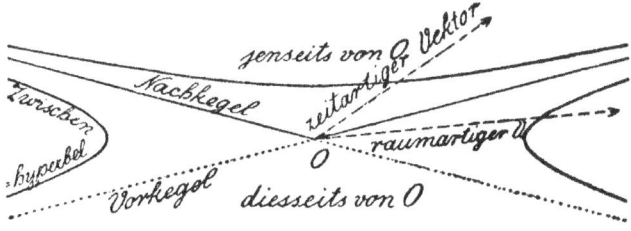

Fig. 22. Albert Einstein and Hermann Minkowski described a curved four-dimensional space-time in 1907.

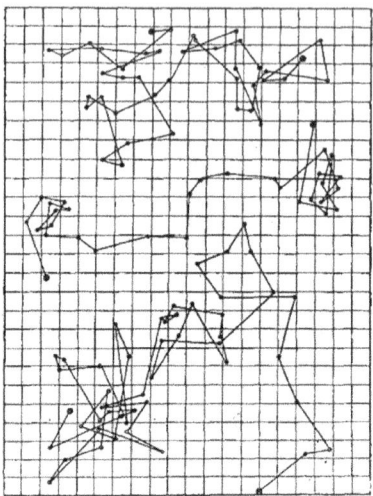

Fig. 23. Jean Baptiste Perrin captured the dance of atoms in 1908.

The radical nonlinearity of this space was only exaggerated by the almost simultaneous proposal that light itself, once believed to be the serene emanation of divine illumination, was a quantum effect. While Jean Baptiste Perrin had finally captured the leaping dance of atoms in 1908 (fig. 23), more or less requiring us to accept the idea that the basic material of the universe takes Bachelier's random or "drunkard's walks,"[28] the new theory of quantum mechanics proposed an even more destabilizing kind of "leaping dance" along the world lines of a warped cosmos—a dance that could apparently never be choreographed, only joined, in a universe in constant flux, in which information and energy are interchangeable and the ultimate nature of reality is never truly grasped.

VIII
The father of the arrow is the thought: how do I expand my reach?
—Paul Klee, *Pedagogical Sketchbook* [29]

In the early twentieth century, the unification of space-time and their critical severance from any fixed form led visual artists into a broad engagement with the visual representation of time and space that would increasingly rely on diagrams.

By 1900, the impetus to produce a depersonalized algebra of signs that could support the messianic and exponential proposals of the nineteenth century seemed irresistible. As Wassily Kandinsky wrote ecstatically from the heat of the crucible, when time and space were collapsing as fast as precision-guided munitions could eliminate them, "the life of the spirit may be fairly represented in [a] diagram."[30] Kazimir Malevich framed his squares with the statement that "the artist who wants to develop his art beyond the potentialities of conventional painting is forced to resort to theory and logic."[31] Erle Loran used diagrams to analyze Paul Cézanne's pictorial structures, Rudolf Laban hoped to inventory the possible movements of the human body in his dance notations, and Paul Klee's *Pedagogical Sketchbook* posited a diagrammatic picture language, a "line on a walk," that can only come to rest "when all arrows are superfluous, it is 'everywhere' and also consequently There!" (fig. 24).[32] In a similar spirit, Friedrich Kiesler would propose "co-realism," a theoretical model with four poles (humans, forms, space, and time), and the logic of form and function that extended from Euclid to the architectural space that Kant had proposed found a home in the Bauhaus, where Hannes Meyer would write, "We examine the daily routine of everyone who lives in the house and this gives us the functional diagram—the functional diagram and the economic programme are the determining principles of the building project."[33]

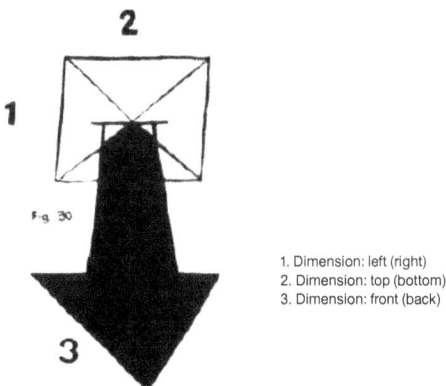

1. Dimension: left (right)
2. Dimension: top (bottom)
3. Dimension: front (back)

Fig. 24. Klee proposed the diagram as the basic factor of all composition.

But although the diagram had apparently freed itself from its eschatological axis in the early nineteenth century, this freedom had come at a price. Even before Einstein, the randomizing effects of two hundred years of industrialized conflict, the constant introduction of new technologies and diverse imports, the rearranging of space and time, and the increased specialization of symbolic languages all affected belief in the long-term validity of an integrated, positional diagram of space and time and replaced it with a disintegrated, juxtapositional diagram of space and time. The emergence of derealization as a widespread clinical condition, closely linked to depersonalization and the ensuing disbelief in the world as a continuous phenomenological whole, can be definitively located in the latter half of the nineteenth century. Centrally planned economies, standardized production, Taylorist and Fordist programs of workplace efficiency all had compartmentalized human relations. Cotard's syndrome, a complex form of schizophrenia where the patient believes they possess an abstract body that is dead, mechanical, or without physical limits was first diagnosed in 1880,[34] and a wide variety of twentieth-century anxieties and mythologies about the apparently discontinuous nature of a supposedly rational reality can be understood as its heirs. The lineage that Alfred H. Barr, Jr. would both diagram and physically realize in his dramatically diagrammatic Museum of Modern Art installations was far closer to the "random walk" of atomic interactions than Barr's better known diagram implies. For every *Bulfinch's Mythology*, there was an Edward Causabon, with his stalled "Key to All Mythologies," for every "Enciclopedia Pedagogica," an absurdist Bouvard and Pécuchet with their "Catalog of Received Ideas," for every Paul Gauguin, with his theory of universal pattern, an Alfred Jarry, dedicated to subverting all such theories. With the collapse of the Euclidian space of the Renaissance diagram, the idea of an ordered access to a unified symbolic space now seemed impossible. The reintroduction of symbolic languages to this space by Carl Jung, and a variety of spiritualists and symbolists encouraged an alternative logic of transpositional elements, radically out of sequence in both time and space. Kiesler himself would soon critique the modernist reduction of home to a diagram of functionality as "the mysticism of hygiene," a skeptical sentiment shared by his collaborator, arch-diagrammaticist Marcel Duchamp.

With the simple addition of an arrow to a dotted line, Duchamp had begun using diagrams as a foundational tool in 1911.[35] Mechanical diagrams allowed Duchamp a new kind of imaginative freedom as their hidden connectivity ultimately became the only stable referent in the construction of a project as scale-free as the world itself, linking animal-machine hybrids and the dimensional isomorphism of *The Large Glass* (1915–23) to the cosmic speculations of *Á l'infinitif* (1963; fig. 25), the so-called White Box where he speculated that a fourth dimension of space might imply our "real" world is only a projection of a higher dimension, an idealist concept that appealed to cubists, futurists, suprematists and surrealists alike.[36]

Under the misnomer "machine drawings," similarly destabilizing diagrammatic connections were critical for Kurt Schwitters's *Merzbau*, Raoul Hausmann, Francis Picabia, Marius de Zayas, and Max Ernst.[37] In an echo of Cotard's syndrome, Duchamp called for a radical depersonalization of art, "a renunciation of all aesthetics,"[38] and firmly located that renunciation in his diagrams, which allowed him to transpose meaning, legibility, scale, and materiality in his unstable pseudo-archive. This effort to imprison chance[39] can be projected in reverse both onto and into the art history of the twentieth century, spiraling into an ever-widening gyre of transpositional sculptural possibilities and ways of assembling pictures, depending on which abductive, bodily, or intellectual stance was adopted. In a characteristically diagrammatic inversion, Duchamp had proposed that by simply transposing the terms *art* and *not-art*, anything could be either.

Formalism, and structuralism and post-structuralism, have all since grappled with the implications of a diagram disconnected from its own symbolic axis and extended through abstract or machinal components. The discontinuity between the proliferation of diagrams that characterized the vastly unequal distribution of risks and resources of the industrial age and their supposedly universalizing intent can be understood as part of a cognitive conflict that continues today, contrasting the dream of a universal diagram against the context of fractured eidetic relations that characterizes the modern mental structure.

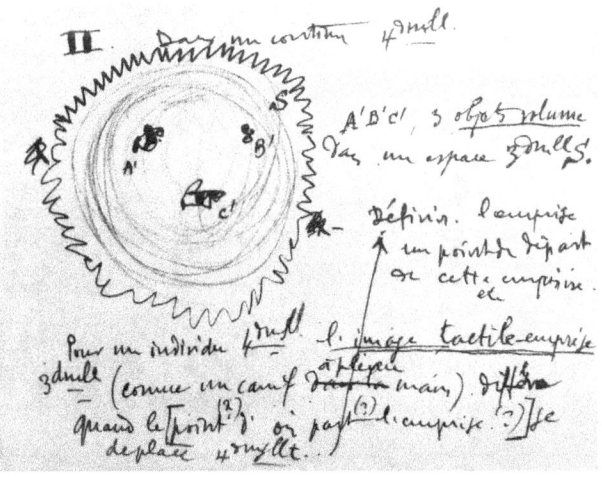

Fig. 25. In Duchamp's *Á l'infinitif*, he speculated about a four-dimensional space.

IX

Non-Euclidean calculus and quantum physics are enough to stretch any brain; and when one mixes them with folklore, and tries to trace a strange background of multi-dimensional reality behind the ghoulish hints of Gothic tales and the wild whispers of the chimney-corner, one can hardly expect to be wholly free from mental tension.
—H. P. Lovecraft, *The Dreams in the Witch House, Weird Tales*, July (Indianapolis: Popular Fiction Publishing Co., 1933).

Quantum mechanics, like Einsteinian space-time cannot be logically inferred from our direct experience of reality. The emergence of a physics without a diagram required a new metaphysics of picture, equally comfortable with obscure proliferations, blank spots, inversions, and juxtapositions. "Fantasy" became the basis for our collective inquiries into the diversity of the universe. After the disturbing psycho-narratives that blossomed from his recombinations of the *Enciclopedia Pedagogica*, Max Ernst had engineered a world of "uncouth angles" in *Let There Be Fashion, Down With Art!* (fig. 26). But the fractured dream logic of surrealism had too many internal inconsistencies to sustain the universal symbolic access it once promised.

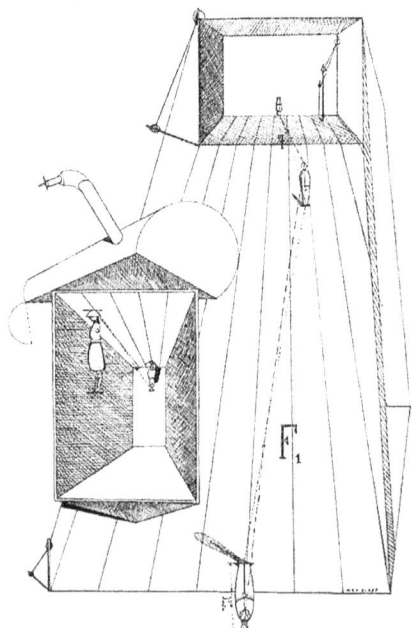

Fig. 26. Max Ernst's *Let There Be Fashion, Down With Art!* engineers a world of "uncouth angles," equivalent to the psycho-geography of his contemporary, H. P. Lovecraft.

Grappling with the possibility of higher dimensions projecting into lower dimensional structures, the psycho-geography of H. P. Lovecraft posited a universal antilogic instead in an attempt to create an new imaginative space, one that might somehow contain quantum mechanics. In much the same way Max Ernst engineered a visual collapse, Lovecraft's horror stories use language to prompt us to search our memories, time itself, for comparisons between the human figure and the universal ground, only to find an expanding space between the psychic landmarks we use to locate ourselves and the universe Lovecraft identifies as indifferent to human concerns or concepts of knowledge.

If Poe was the first true scientific fiction author, constructing a logic of imagination, then H. P. Lovecraft was the first true "weird realist," a term critical in our effort to trace the diagram past the boundaries of the messianically logical forms proposed by the Bauhaus and Vkhutemas and to reassert its claim to universal applicability, even in the non-Euclidian spaces of the twentieth century.

In *Weird Realism: Lovecraft and Philosophy*, philosopher Graham Harman details how Lovecraft's precisely nuanced relations between object and background, or "ontography," allows him to develop a convincingly "allusive weirdness" that allows him to reintroduce the concept of "demons" (the Cthulhu mythos) and support them as narratively plausible as a direct consequence of their orientation between "the normal" object, or figure, and the background.[40]

For Michel Houellebecq, this quality of Lovecraft's writing is distinctly architectural, as "one discovers architecture from a variety from angles, one moves within it."[41] For Houllebecq, Lovecraft "is the first writer to have discovered the poetic impact of topography,"[42] combining the multiform descriptive methods of science to generate a vertiginous literature, for "without the juxtaposition of the minute and the limitless, the punctual and the infinite, there can be no vertigo."[43] But it is not the classical logic of Kant's "schema" that supports Peirce and Poe, it is "uncouth," non-Euclidean. In *The Gods of H. P. Lovecraft*, Donald Tyson summarizes the function of Lovecraft's Yog-Sothoth, the engendering proliferator of his nonhuman topology. "In the higher worlds above our own which is the world of real things there is a gatekeeper . . . capable of opening gates to higher worlds… with certain uncouth angles."[44] For Lovecraft, the diagram is not only occupied by demons, it is built by them. Like Foucault's "hidden carrier," Lovecraft's Sothoth bends two human imaginary spaces, language and time. As in Blake's writing, widely separated categorical terms are vigorously collided, inducing a rhapsodic confusion familiar from biblical, alchemical, and political tracts, but Lovecraft creates a different kind of intermediate zone, a diagonal disassociation of the dimensional isomorphism between allusive and eidetic spaces similar to Husserl's separation of space from time and similarly ambiguous in intent. Paradoxically, the distant and impersonal author relies on a collapse of meaning, distance, and time to dramatize our bodily awareness of the induced disassociation. For Harman, Lovecraft's project is rendered isomorphic through its specific use of local conventions of narrative and language, forcing us to progress along the semiotic axis that Peirce labels "abduction," or what we might call guesswork.

For an artist like Blake, it may be precisely the progress that their work makes along this axis and away from the original index that constitutes its true "sensual objecthood." But in Lovecraft's work, our movement along the abductive axis is placed under an insufferable tension, as the process of human-oriented abduction is warped toward a nonhuman pole. By bending language and time, Lovecraft creates a kind of diagonal disassociation, reversing human categories of true and false—at least by the standards of his time.

Lovecraft's anti-Blakean mythos is notable in another specifically diagrammatic way. In a resolution of the dilemma discussed earlier, it is both profoundly introverted and shareable. Explored by many of Lovecraft's own correspondents, the Cthulu mythos has since been expanded by multiple writers over the last century, remaining largely true to its central conceits while introducing a more comprehensive philosophy of being than Lovecraft's reflexive misanthropy.

Most recently, Reza Negarestani's *Cyclonopedia* collides with the narrative complexity of H. P. Lovecraft's cosmology, "Where radical openness subverts the logic of capacity from within,"[45] embracing the principle of constant diagrammatic inversion and the implied diminution of human import that was so horrific for Lovecraft but recombining it with a series of new diagrams including one "of n-dimensions,"[46] creating a parallel Lovecraftian horror-mythology from a non-Western perspective that similarly stipulates "an unground, a shadow outside time and space."[47]

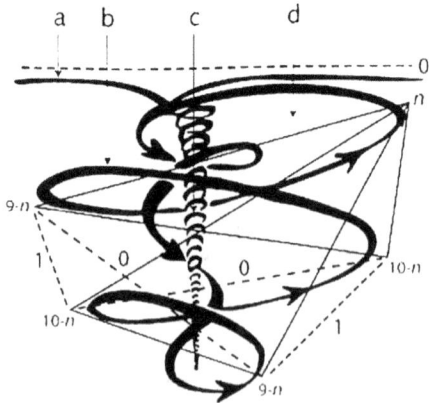

Fig. 27. The Infernotron. A contemporary diagram of Lovecraft's fictional shared cosmogony.

X

In 1946, it turned out that quantum mechanics was not so undiagrammable after all. Lovecraft's temperamental opposite, the gregarious, bongo-playing genius Richard Feynman emerged in the postwar period as the "Great Explainer," developing a solution to the "random walk" called a path integral, an integrated solution to all the paths that might be taken, as if one could take all the walks at once. To publicly demystify the confusing bestiary of particles and interactions, to corral their diverse world lines and collapse an illimitable proliferation into a limited scope, Feynman needed to create an entirely new kind of diagram, one that integrates multiple possible subatomic particle reactions into a single diagrammatic body (fig. 28).

So effective and mutable is the Feynman diagram as a scientific tool, it might be easy to mistake its functionality for a basic condition of informational space. But the diagram (a diagram, all diagrams) is neither a simple expression of the terms of the space it occupies, nor simply a useful metaphor for a hidden bridge between the local manifolds or ordering systems and the proliferation of localized difference that constitutes the primary operating system of conscious thought. It is something more than a translator. As Manuel DeLanda has noted, a diagram contains all of its possible expressions, and the inventorying of natural properties may be suddenly and effectively replaced by a higher order of unity.[48] The infinite abyss of Lovecraft's Cthulu mythos can become just one of the seventeen stages of Joseph Campbell's 1949 monomyth diagram. Through a precise definition of inherent topological relations and force relations, new diagrams like these can ultimately produce a radical reduction of local complexity and a corresponding increase in accessibility. So the table can be both system and diagram.

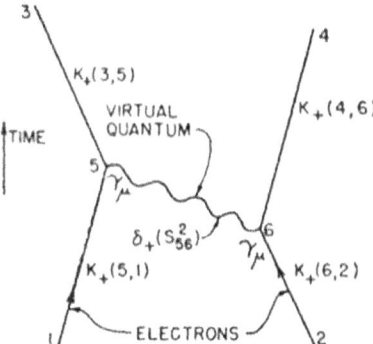

Fig. 28. A Feynman diagram integrates multiple possible subatomic particle reactions into a single diagrammatic space.

By proposing new conventions of dimensional connection across the infinite sheet, such exploratory diagrams also reinvigorate theories of picture and the possibilities of agency within them. It is through these diagrams that the profound questions of relative time, scale, distance, gauge symmetry, proximity, and imagined immunity from discontinuity and relationality that define our use of any shared informational space become evident.

Broadcasting the unruly electrons that Feynman had tamed across radio and television networks, the feedback diagrams of Cold War cybernetics characterized the ruthlessly pragmatic "command and control" philosophy of the nuclear states, retracting from the symbolic axis of nature along the axes of animal-machine communications and systems theory that nonetheless supported fundamental research such as Feynman's as an existential necessity. At the same time, the conceptual axis of set theory and Riemannian topology was being extended, positing another diagrammatic definition of universal possibility against the vast nullity of Lovecraftian n-dimensional space, an image of reality so alien that it required a new theory of picture once again.

How the connections between these isomorphic manifolds of increasing abstraction continue to grow is shown in Max Tegmark's diagrammatic classifications of formal systems.[49] For Tegmark, the scientific pursuit of higher and higher orders of formal abstraction definitively does not necessarily point toward a final Theory of Everything. Rather, each generation of diagrams offers radically new perspectives on local nature.

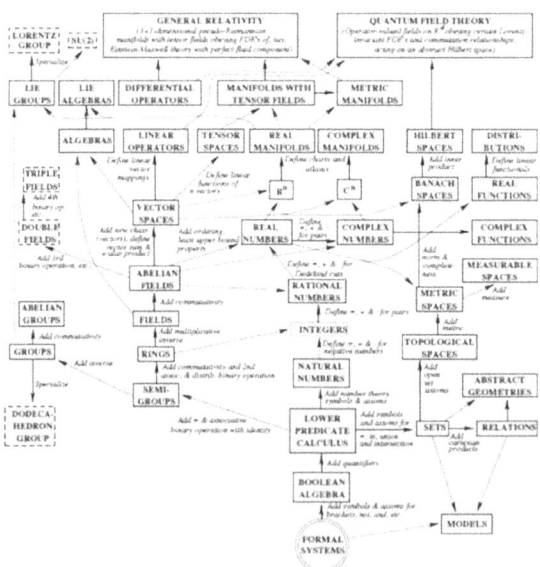

Fig. 29. Tegmark shows the relationships between various mathematical structures. The full tree is probably infinite.

XI

Postwar existentialism, politicized by Jean-Paul Sartre and given ontological status by Heidegger and Husserl, provided a context for the appearance of this next theory of picture, along with new analogical and artistic bodies that could successfully orient themselves toward the recently exposed infinities of time, space, and mass destruction without either falling into the hygienic mythography of modernism or denying the ungrounded cosmography of post-Einsteinian space. For Gilles Deleuze, analogy could be embodied as language by passing through a kind of diagram, which he refers to as a form of "catastrophe." Focusing on the work of Francis Bacon, who called his swipes and scrubs "diagrams" in the postwar period, Deleuze writes, "for Bacon the diagram must remain limited in space and time, it must remain operative . . . and the operation of the diagram is to introduce possibilities of fact . . . not the fact itself . . . The diagram does not act as a code but as a modulator,"[50] and he calls this tempered diagram *a middle way*, a term strongly reminiscent of Molina's Middle Knowledge. Stjernfelt similarly notes that, "the naked, easy-to-grasp diagram rarely occurs in art,"[51] and characterizes the diagram as a form of hypostatic abstraction in which any painting or sketch always indexes another group of terms, even as it moves away from it. "Diagrammatical experimentation is . . . only made possible by gaining access to a landscape by means of a body."[52] Bacon's demonic, sectioned figures are diagrams, as are the frames and structures that define them. These readings complicate the conventional understanding of the landscape as passive and the body as active or causal. The diagram is the generator and interpreter of this topology or body, capable of being read both as an emergent quality and as a sensual object, fantasy, and factuality. With the discovery of DNA in 1953, the body and the diagram become fused as active, causal terms—the diagram of the double helix representing life itself (fig. 30).

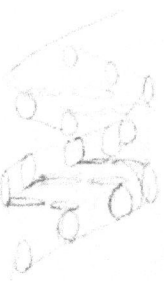

Fig. 30. With the discovery of DNA in 1953, the body and the diagram become fused and folded around active, causal terms—the diagram of life.

Diagrams not only bring ideas into proximity through their bodies, where the intensities of localized forces define their expression, they both superimpose and superpose them, opening the way for us to move freely from Bacon's diagrams to DNA to Deleuze's philosophical diagrams and accept the centrality of diagrammatic thinking to the imagination—the mode of inquiry that Peirce called abduction, with all its gothic overtones of being "taken." This incorporeal, roving body provides the promise and the reality of an environment in which we can endlessly vary the terms of what Husserl calls fantasy, in that fantasy "shares the picture's relation to its subject, defined by similarity and variation, while, on the other hand, fantasy seems, just like perception, to take place directly and without any intermediary."[53]

Deleuze distinguished two other types of painting as diagrams, each with its own bodily form. Purely geometric optical abstraction, acting a symbolic code for a Kantian spiritual schema, reduced the chaotic proliferation of possibilities to a minimum, while abstract expressionism extended the fullest chaotic potential of a spatially ungrounded, bodiless diagram to the spatial and temporal whole of the painting, forming "a continuum going in all dimensions simultaneously, beyond the literal dimensions of any work," as Allan Kaprow put it.[54] At the same time, as Brian O'Doherty noted, "The all-over drip pictures . . . seem to articulate a question from the missing artist: 'Where am I?'"[55] For Kaprow, this depersonalization optimized the blurring of art and life, reorienting Peirce's diagrammatic pragmatics towards cultural engagement, opening up the contextual space for what Kaprow called "Un-Art," a lifelong effort to realize the drunkard's walk, one step at a time.

In music, the question of where, or even who the artist was, became quickly intertwined with the problem of chance, leading to more chance- and performance-based systems like the open-form diagram scores of composer Earle Brown, which influenced Karlheinz Stockhausen and John Cage. In the postwar period, several theories describing dramatic variations in transitional phenomena began to hint that more complex processes were underway emerged. Catastrophe theory, which emerged in the 1960s, maps degenerating critical points of complex systems, with a central fold or cusp forming around the point at which the entire system collapses (fig. 31); for Deleuze, this fold, or catastrophe, is a concept critical to the operation of the diagram in Bacon's work. Through the diagram, painting recovers its analogical body, one that is neither purely optical nor purely manual and chaotic. Bacon's Lovecraftian figures are torqued and folded around a diagram that constitutes the true body of the painting, outlining the geometry of the existential abyss without ever quite falling in. Echoing Peirce, Deleuze would later call his overall diagrammatic theory "pragmatics,"[56] a discipline with the now almost-inevitable four components; the generative tracing, the transformative map of the tracings, the

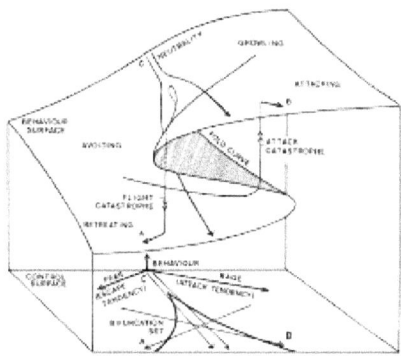

Fig. 31. Catastrophe theory, which emerged in the 1960s, maps degenerating critical points of complex systems, with a central fold or cusp forming around the point at which the entire system collapses.

diagram of the map, and the final component, a "program" that will both semiotize and physicalize the content, allowing the cycle to begin again.

In the 1970s, chaos theorists began to examine supposedly deterministic systems that are highly sensitive to initial conditions such as the weather. Even though the future behavior of these systems should be able to be fully determined, they are predictable only for a while and then appear to become random. Chaos theory could not be diagrammed before the development of the computer, as the iterations of its paths were too complex to produce by hand, and the iconic diagram of chaos theory, the strange attractor called the Lorenz Butterfly, is a snapshot of the evolving path of a dynamic system. The wings of the butterfly represent small changes in the initial condition of the system, which can cause a chain of events leading to large-scale phenomena familiar to devotees of time-travel movies. Like a Feynman diagram, this drawing synthesizes multiple layers of information, summing up the difficulties faced by both Laplace's "intellect" and Maxwell's "demon," even while solving them (fig. 32).

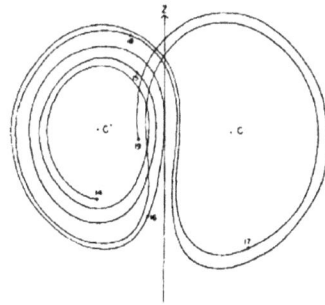

Fig. 32. The iconic diagram of chaos theory, the strange attractor called the Lorenz Butterfly.

XII

Central to these highly fluid diagrams is an increased acceptance that metamorphic concepts of threshold and flux are integral to both physical and logical systems. The implication that a human presence might be only one of many causal elements in a composition was fertile ground for the Fluxus movement with its emphasis on contingency. For Joseph Beuys, as for Kaprow, art was public play. As his pedagogy became social sculpture, the public execution of the diagram became metonymic with proof of concept. The diagram, presented by Beuys as the iconic symbol of "experimental" form, became experiential. Although Feynman would have derided Beuys's theories of energy as "cargo cult science," building on Rudolf Steiner's theosophical and pedagogical diagrams, Beuys exploited his diagrammatic biographical-analogical language to capitalize on symbolic connections between mind and body, the human world and the ancestral realms, joining the politics of energy to the dimension of pure forms, teaching us how to become diagrams.

In an effort to review some part of this long history of diagrammatic strategies and directly connect them to present-day practices, in 2013 I curated an exhibition in New York also called *The Temptation of the Diagram*.[57] What became immediately evident from the range of diagram projects on view were the advantages and the price for such apparent liberation. While Mel Bochner's work consistently proposed the diagram as directly equivalent to its execution in real space (fig. 34) and equally logical diagrams were essential to the practice of artists like Alice Aycock and Robert Smithson, escape vectors for a world performed, enacted, and explored were being diagrammed in the works of Carolee Schneemann, the de-compositional arrangements of sculptors

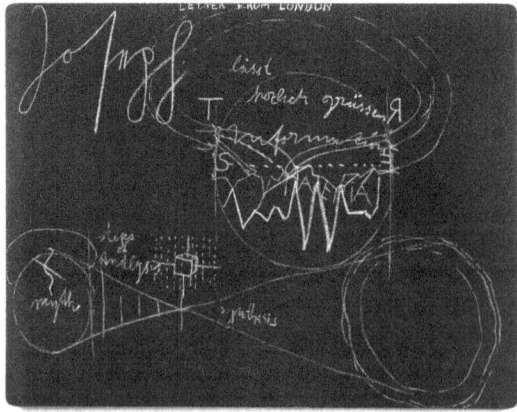

Fig. 33. For Beuys, the diagram was metonymic with the proof of concept.

Barry Le Va and Lygia Clark, and in the movement graphs of Yvonne Rainier and Trisha Brown, where vocabularies of pure form are unfurled, folded, and re-formed across sound, space, and time. In a diagram, the distinction between reality and unreality, between connection and conspiracy, is as thin as the paper the diagram is drawn on. Although Bochner himself carefully distinguished between "finished drawings; working drawings; diagrammatic drawings" in his 1969 exhibition essay "Anyone Can Learn to Draw,"[58] and Bernice Rose and Ann Temkin try to differentiate between the "diagrams" and the various types of drawings, blackboards, and lists in *Thinking Is Form: The Drawings of Joseph Beuys*, the diagram resists historical inclusion and overwhelms its own boundaries.[59] Incomplete or not, each generation of diagrams incorporates the previous era and becomes the substrate for the next. Diagrams not only describe reality but also in some sense enlarge it, simply by coming into being.

Artists' diagrams of universal conditions present themselves publicly with ludic confidence and apophenic connectivity, simultaneously encouraging limit-case thinking and a hermetic withdrawal from the conventional taxonomy of the world. Capitalizing on its properties as universal translator, Peircian abduction-deduction-intuition machine, fantasy generator, and "thing-in-itself," the artists' diagram as model-of-thought manifests the final fantasy of omnidirectional potency. Rhapsodic thinking, quasi-science, suspicious topologies, and mathematical inconsistencies can all be elided with a confident group of gestures and terms. There is no requirement for rationality, only mutuality—or isomorphism of parts. As Gilles Deleuze wrote, "a diagram is a map, or rather several superimposed maps. And from one diagram to the next, new maps are drawn."[60] As for Flaubert's anchorite saint, so for these artists; the final temptation, "to assume all forms," became irresistible.

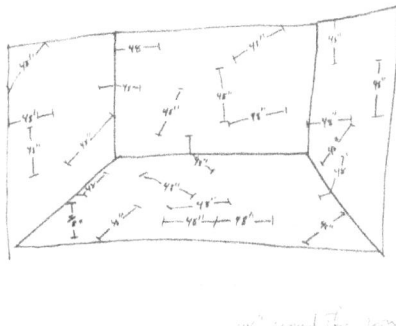

Fig. 34. Mel Bochner's diagram for *48" Around the Room*, 1969, proposes the diagram's meaning as being equivalent to its execution in real space.

XIII

With Beuys, the messianic artistic diagrammatic program that had begun in earnest in 1900 reached a plateau, as the world became increasingly diagrammed as a potential space for art, a dialectical process culminating, in art historical terms, in the Vierergruppe diagram of Rosalind Krauss, presented in her famous structuralist essay of 1976, "Sculpture in the Expanded Field," an effort to look at the entire art historical process "from the point of view of logical structure."[61] This is the diagram that has defined art practice in my lifetime, so I hope you can forgive me if we spend some time with it (fig. 35).

At the time, "logical structure" seemed to mean the production of vast, sometimes inspired, inventories of "logical" or "axiomatic" forms—inventories which might programmatically lead human consciousness into Kant's mathematical sublime. As Krauss puts it: "It follows, then, that within any one of the positions generated by the given logical space, many different mediums might be employed. It follows as well that any single artist might occupy, successively, any one of the positions. And it also seems the case that within the limited position of sculpture itself the organization and content of much of the strongest work will reflect the condition of the logical space."[62] At the time of its production, artistic practice was still largely understood in Krauss's postmodern terminology as existing along varying succeeding and oppositional cultural axes, such as identity, sexuality, and appropriation, and Krauss relies on the art historical notion of successive artistic positions (rather than juxtapositions or transposition),[63] arguing that her diagram presents a "universe of terms that are felt to be in opposition within a cultural situation."

But it is there, in the notion that it is actually organized information (or logic), that underlies the terms of the expanded field, that the diagram becomes truly prophetic. The most significant and direct consequence of the full and logical exploration of any given space and the conflation of material and information is not that any one kind of axiomatic or logical forms are a "stronger" reflection of the space, it is that logically, an inventory of all possible forms, including both the logically axiomatic forms of Andre, Holt, or Judd and the highly expressive, idiosyncratic, chaotic, folded, catastrophic, but equally axiomatic forms generated by chance, nature, and time, is the strongest reflection of the condition—as the vast projects of Gerhard Richter and Sigmar Polke and the subsequent careers of Frank Stella and Sol LeWitt would eloquently testify. As Krauss noted, any single artist might occupy successively any one of the positions, or as it turned out, all of them. This critical juncture is also where we find Lippard's "art as idea and art as action" connecting to the outer edge of the nominated field of "sculpture" to include other given fields of human facture, connecting and reorienting that redefinition to the entire field of art practice. Through this diagram the chained legacy

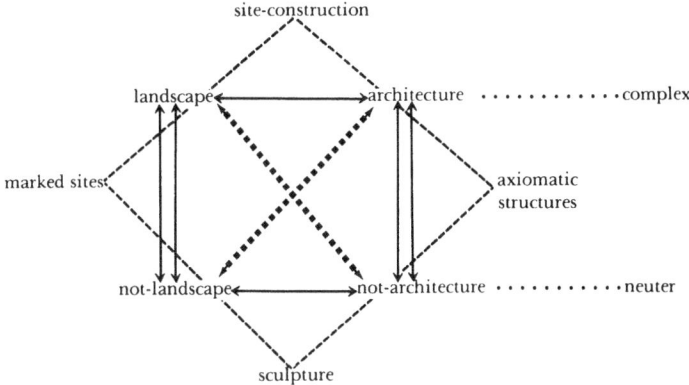

Fig. 35. Krauss's diagram allows that "any single artist might occupy, successively, any one of the positions."

of the tree diagrams of Barr, the art trees of Ad Reinhardt, Kaprow's Happenings and the combinatorial logics of Fluxus, diagrammed by George Maciunas and Dick Higgins would all be absorbed into Sol LeWitt's totalizing statement, "The process is mechanical and should not be tampered with. It should run its course."[64]

Almost before the ink was dry on Krauss's essay, a succession of pseudo-movements such as neo-expressionism, neo-geo, identity art, abject art, etc., sought to programmatically exploit the successive possibilities of just such an expanded field, often supported by claims relating to notions of oppositional cultural axes. In the 1980s, a vast array of recompositional works juxtaposed the symbolic dream languages of surrealism with the formal terms of postminimalism and pop in a succession of hybrid movements. But in retrospect (and not surprisingly given their surrealist antecedents), the successive movements can be more properly understood as running their cultural terms in parallel, not in opposition. The ensuing collapse of the distinction between information and material would fuse the art world with the world itself, orienting both toward a new matrix of cultural axes, based not only on the sequence of position, succession, juxtaposition, and opposition but also on multiple positions, superpositions, and aggregations that would redefine the terms expansion and field. In other words, Krauss's diagram articulates not just the erosion of formal terms but of opposition between form and content, anticipating cultural and technical developments related to the emergence of the first truly global diagram, the Internet.

XIV

The Internet began as an effort to connect terminals at four institutions, as shown in this simple diagram from 1969 (fig. 36). The World Wide Web is the informational network the Internet hosts, with the distinction becoming less and less clear each year as the two networks grow together. Its central requirement was that information be not only transmittable but translatable by an potentially infinite ensemble of physically diverse networks. If information was our cultural DNA, it would need a transcription process to be read into the proliferation of forms yet to come. Its expansion into consumer-grade computational spaces and their occupation and mediation by interconnected human and nonhuman information systems has comprehensively expanded the definition of the field of cultural production and its diagrammatic relationships. Although this redefinition of the field is still in process, it extends to all areas of the human project that can be mediated by computational space, and to date no human activity has been discovered that cannot be mediated by computational space.

Growing from that first interconnection of four computers, the information complex, the hidden substrate and indexical basis of contemporary culture, is an extraordinary composite, an aggregation of diagrams built from trillions of highly ordered diagrams of microstates that physically integrate quantum force relations, ceaselessly following the cheapest possible energy paths through a network. Throughout the network, multiple ordinators, demons, and intellects craft, secure, and compete for the letters and images we see formed from lines of code and patterns of electrons—a hive-like architecture of pure energy that carries every form of symbolic communication. Computational space itself has no meaningful aesthetic, only a series of nested workspaces whose overall appearance is the haphazard result of legacy coding and commercial guesswork. The screen replaces the endless plane of diagrammatic space with the slippery ice sheet of fragmented and stuttering digital connectivity. It may be wide ranging but it is not informationally deep. As a point of comparison, the equivalent of a zettabyte of data, equal to the entire Internet traffic of the planet in 2015, could be stored within one kilogram of DNA.

Despite the familiar complaint of information overload, the humanly experienced Web largely compresses what we already know into degraded "sensory appearances," and what is often described as image saturation might be more accurately understood as the mechanical repetition of a range of visual phenomena specifically designed to attract and retain a small part of human attention. But the active components of this network cannot be meaningfully counted. The number of connected devices now far exceeds the number of human beings on earth while both the human and object-to-object force relations that sustain it (temporal, physical, political, and environmental) are increasingly hidden.

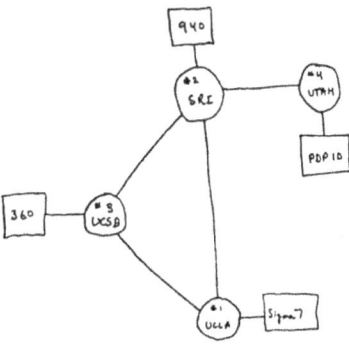

Fig. 36. The first known diagram of the World Wide Web, 1969.

For artists of the previous century who were often deeply concerned with representation, Vilém Flusser's description of the camera as a "black box" whose program expanded synchronously with the appearance of new images was immensely useful. But that instrument is intrinsically different from the black box of computational space that anticipates and promotes desire through aggressively predictive programming of the subject. The traditional subject, previously examined retroactively, is becoming a predictive profile, both aggregated and distributed in form and continuously reconstituted as a proprietary data trail. Driven by biometrics and marketing algorithms, legislated by unread user agreements and secret courts, the spectral geometries and datascapes of the oikumene are already too many, too large, too small, too cumulative, and too ephemeral to be understood in the space and time of the human look. In 1991, Bruno Latour named these hybrid forms "quasi-objects," defined the ongoing cultural result of this process as "hyper-incommensurability," and diagrammed the relations of objects and people inside this condition as "actor-network theory" (fig. 37).[65] Although Latour dates this process to at least as far back as Kant's compartmentalized diagram, it is hard to imagine it being as persuasive without the physical example of humans interacting with the networks of the Internet.

As I came of age as an artist in 1995, operating under the logic of this infinitely connective, globalized, transactional information system, it became apparent that any single artist trying to explore the underlying nature of the expanded field had to simultaneously consider their relationship not only in terms of "opposed positions in sequence" (postmodernist in Krauss's terms), but in terms of occupying multiple positions in parallel (multipositionality). Eagerly anticipating further stages in Latour's process of development, artists of my generation began to seek out strategies of reciprocal multipositioning through the network

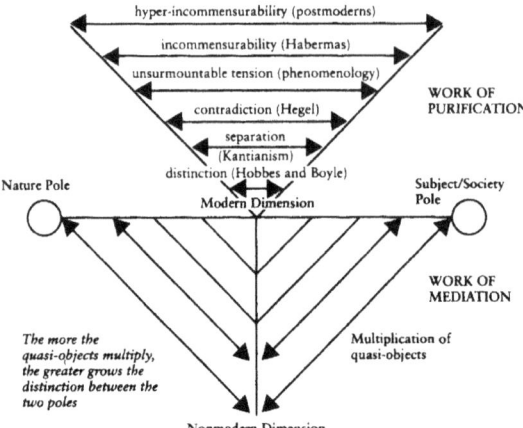

Fig. 37. Bruno Latour calls hybrid informational/material forms quasi-objects and defines the result of their multiplication as hyper-incommensurability.

sometimes grouped together under the category of relational aesthetics (or "multiple positions in relation"). In the terms I have been using here, relational aesthetics can be described as a variant of multipositional practice with only one significant inclusion: its positions are occupied partly in relation to the expanded definition of public space proposed by Kaprow and Krauss and partly in relation to the cultural and productive space that emerged along with the Internet (fig. 38).

The connectively multipositional projects of the 1990s were followed by their own logical successors, micropositional or "archival" projects that presented tightly edited informational sequences as complete models. Once the access to the symbolic axis that was restored by multipositional artists in the 1990s was extended to the indiscriminately inclusive superarchive of the World Wide Web, its infinite capacity fostered a sense of ahistorical anomie. This archival impulse, which located a highly anthropocentric version of alterity in specific cultural chronologies, was in turn displaced by the energetically sprawling and ostensibly de-positional works that occupy many positions in superficially arbitrary or incomplete sequences, a generic and formless aggregation.

If abstract expressionism could be very loosely described as Jungian archetypes given ontological and phenomenological depth by the diagrams of Martin Heidegger and Edmond Husserl and expressed through the hands of artists, then contemporary art—socially expressive yet technically abstracted and politically mute—might be characterized as a combination of the flattening structure of the Internet, which exchanges the volumetric space of Newton and the space time of Einstein for a kind for de-spatialized time and apparent instantaneity, with the ontological flatness described by speculative realists such as Harman, expressed through the glowing windows and trained responses to the permitted action chains of programs such as Photoshop. Since the introduction of personal computers, handmade diagrams have tellingly begun to vanish from the visual toolkit of artists and architects, only to be replaced by the invisible traces of programming diktats. The individual artist working in the studio and the components of cultural production are interchangeable. Given the growing reliance of contemporary art culture on computational management systems, performance metrics, and financial engineering, the stealthy but steady emergence of an essentially eidetic or algorithmic art culture makes further review of underlying concepts of the diagram all the more urgent. The concepts of network, distribution, and hub have become central to art historical presentation, exemplified in MoMA's now-iconic art historical network created for the exhibition *Inventing Abstraction, 1910–1925*. The messianic hopes of the contemporary avant-garde, once made immanent by Kandinsky and Malevich, are now compressed into websites like *e-flux*, *Contemporary Art Daily*, and *Artsy*. If the goal for John Cage, among many others, was an art that rivaled nature in its refusal of intentionality, we arrived instead at a continuously presentational environment, an Adorno-esque performance of knowledge that simulates chance only in its foreclosure of mutuality. Since the components of this network cannot be individualized, even Duchamp's careful juxtaposition of antithetical components (or purportedly antipositional diagramming) cannot be aesthetically implemented. Where Duchamp once proposed art could be anything, now it could, must, be everything.

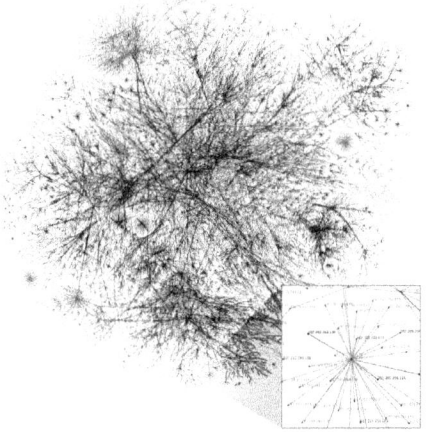

Fig. 38. The Internet, the first truly global diagram.

XV

The wide-ranging field of research known as network theory, pioneered by Albert-László Barabási, describes how this entire process is found in almost every connective system (fig. 39). If an unexpected success of Krauss's diagram was that it introduced a radically poststructural vocabulary of forms, then poststructuralism's own failure was to understand that its own particular local nature was still bound by the laws of time and entropy. Nothing, whether it is information, energy, or matter, is ever truly lost, but everything must change. In this essential aspect, the dual nature of the diagram, as fixed table and mobile vector, perfectly complements the first and second laws of thermodynamics. Network theory proposes innate limits to the number of connections that can occur in a physically connected or networked system. It is important to note this is a function that has nothing to do with the actual content of the network. Any networked system, like the Internet, the human brain, or third stage capitalism, will follow these laws. Not only is there an upper limit to the number of complex, interdependent ideas that can populate a network efficiently (even a human one, as shown by the Human Connectome Project), but as the system grows, the need for efficient information processing creates "hubs" to avoid an endless series of random walks. These informationally dense hubs constitute a so-called rich club,[66] creating what is called the "bow-tie" effect. Who said theorists don't have a sense of humor?

Barabási's theory takes special note that the information being carried, like all systems, is subject to the laws of entropy. In 2010, a team of physicists under Shoichi Toyabe even built the demon proposed by

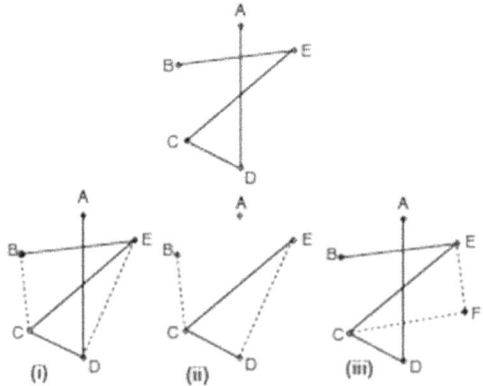

Fig. 39. Barabási's network theory proposes laws that control the number of connections that can occur in a networked system. All connective systems must evolve by adding nodes.

Maxwell and conclusively demonstrated that information could be transmuted into energy.[67] Information (or noumena), energy, and matter (or phenomena), are interchangeable. "Form" and "content" are the same thing, namely, information, and do not enjoy any inherent oppositions at any scale.

The third law of thermodynamics states that the more entropy is introduced into any system, even one composed of pure information, the more homogenous it becomes, even as it spreads. The information hubs compete with each other, with the most successful dominating the system, increasing its homogeneity. As the system approaches higher levels of interconnectedness, it becomes more and more self-similar. Under the right conditions, just four conditions will be enough to produce synchronization and stabilize a system into a lockstep pattern. As if this was not enough, Barabási's research goes on to describe even more exotic potential results. At low enough temperatures, complex information states enter a quantum state called "superposition," wherein atoms not only occupy the same space, but begin to share their very being, becoming more and more like each other until they essentially behave as a single entity, called a Bose-Einstein condensate. Atoms are held in multiple quantum states, physically superposed not over each other but within each other, as a superpositional state emerges (fig. 40).[68]

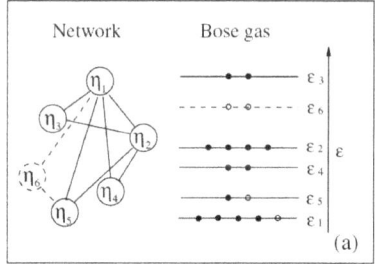

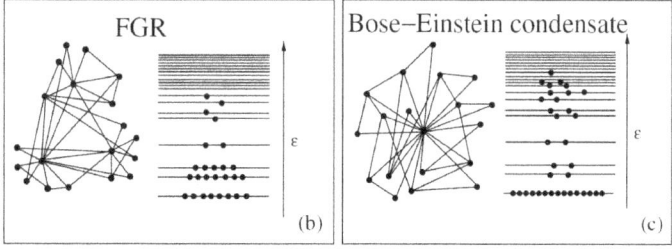

Fig. 40. Networks undergo phase shifts at certain levels of complexity, and the number of energy levels and particles increases linearly with time. In the Bose-Einstein condensate mode, the fittest node attracts a fraction of all the links.

Figure 41 applies this thermodynamic concept to the idea of a cultural network, diagramming a positional sequence that includes all the phases mentioned earlier in the essay. Starting at the top, the compartmentalized space of Aristotelian and medieval cosmology transitions to the systemic space of the Renaissance and then to the positionality of Newton's "system of the world." Beginning in the eighteenth century, Latour's process of "hyperincommensurability" produces more and more quasi-objects, resulting in phases of juxtaposition, transposition, and opposition. As the network creates more and more connections, and produces more and more quasi-objects, the logic of position, opposition, and multiposition can no longer be organized around a universe of terms in opposition. Decompositional, micropositional, and relational works emerge as introverted variants of multipositionality. As the network condenses, even the ideas of form and content can no longer be usefully separated within this overall matrix. As global knowledge systems respond to the flattening incentives of the attention complex, all individual experiences are more rapidly processed by centralized hubs, homogenized within hierarchical networks of presentation and "superposed" within the information matrix. As data is repeatedly and widely shared, the information complex becomes more similar overall, an effect inevitably accelerated by innate availability and confirmation biases. Over time the aggregated database itself becomes a kind of echo chamber where varying terms are simply activated within a variable commutative space, a matrix of all possible choices.

Is this what Sotirios Bahtsetzis calls the "deterritorialization" of aesthetic judgment, once inherent to the diagrammatic impulse in Kandinsky, Malevich, and Ernst, and then formalized by Krauss? Certainly, the Internet has contributed to a cultural homogeneity not found since the first ideograms. As these diagrammatic force relations of networks become increasingly predictable and our own responses become more and more conditioned to the limited options within it, will this highly programmed and increasingly predictable computational environment come to "know" us better than we will ever know ourselves? Hypothetically, the complete inventory of forms offered could ultimately be expressed through an integral, a presentation of the full spectrum of order and chaos, control and expression. It might even be something like Llull's *Ars Magna* or the Glass Bead Game[69] described by Herman Hesse at the onset of the information age. This would signal an end, or at least a superpositional completion, of art conceived through eidetic connections.

It would be ironic, indeed, if the most diagram-dependent system engineered in human history turned out to be the final iteration of the diagram. But no logical system or individual is static, or exclusive; all oscillate constantly, acquiring new identities and passing through multiple phase shifts. Network theory can be successfully extrapolated

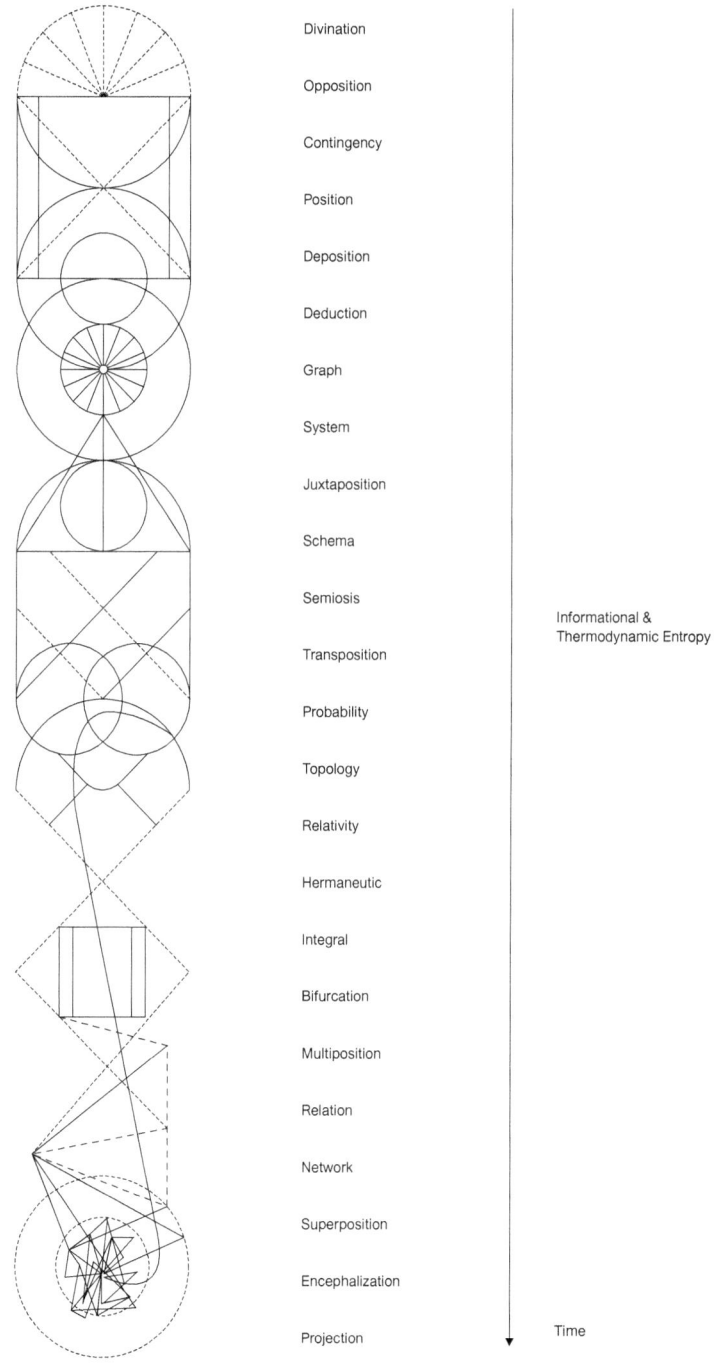

Fig. 41. The progression from divination to projection.

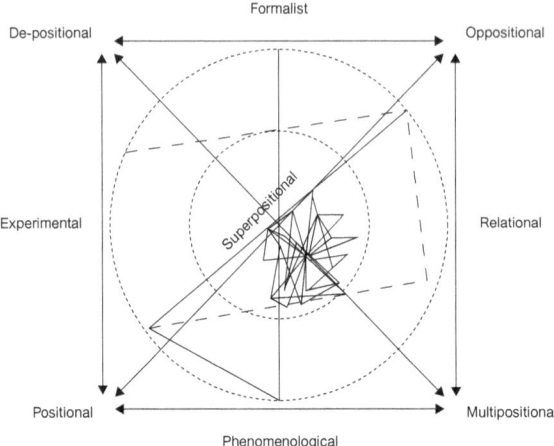

Fig. 42. All types of positionality are included in the superpositional matrix of forms.

to model atomic networks or predict the location of cell phone users and the formation of networks between galaxies. However, even within network theory, there are strong limits to prediction. As we have seen before, a characteristic of diagrams is their ability to suddenly replace any system, no matter how vast, with a visualization of higher orders of unity. For a discipline whose basis is the movement away from the index and toward the proliferation of meanings, surely the only unacceptable trajectory is a too complete belief in the current diagram, one that would abandon its exploratory modes and become fixed into the rules of discourse. To avoid this, Barabási's theory demands that we consider new perspectives, from outside the network, where those limits can be countered through the creation of new diagrammatic bodies.

XVI

The pursuit of a new diagrammatic body that can explore philosophy, art, and science, a human product capable of a nonhuman perspective, the implausible in pursuit of the impossible, leads us next to philosopher Graham Harman's diagram, "The Quadruple Object" from 2012 (fig. 43). Since diagrams initiate a vertical disassociation between informational space and real space, and have a theoretically infinite capacity for extension by proposing new conventions of connection—isomorphism in many directions—it is only to be expected that a philosopher like Harman, who is positively oriented toward research, vertical isomorphism, overlay, and connection, would have to produce a diagram that attempts to unify all aspects of human perception.

Unlike many earlier exclusionary diagrams, Harman attempts to include several purportedly incompatible things at once. He proposes ten possible links between four modes or properties, shown in circles, through which any "object" perceives any other "object." Together they form what Harman calls the quadruple object. By "object," Harman means "everything," at every scale, including ideas, which he calls "real qualities," perceived things, which he calls "sensual objects," and feelings, which he calls "sensual qualities." These are the three poles addressed in the diagrams of Edmund Husserl and Charles S. Peirce. The fourth pole, the one he calls the realm of "real objects," constitutes the inherently unreachable true nature of objects, and *finitude* is the term Harman uses to describe the impossibility of any object fully decoding any other object. Critical to appreciating this diagram is remembering that all modes are always present at all times, if not always equally accessible. The universe, quarks, the word *Internet*, lost train tickets, your first love, elections, dinosaur blood, this text,

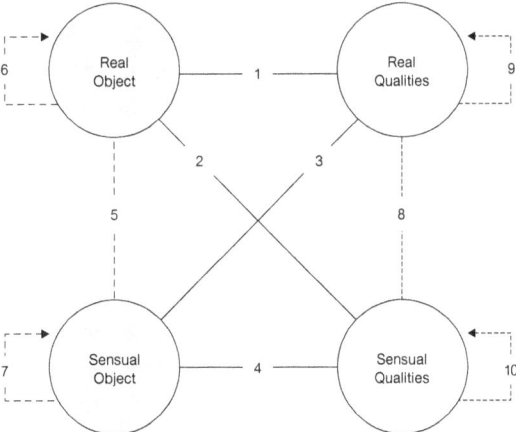

Fig. 43. Considered as an icon, Harman's "Ten Possible Links" can be read as both image and metaphor, referring back to its own ontology through the intermediary of itself.

set theory, fire, SAT results, the Getty Research Institute, fourteenth-century Paris, and Graham Harman himself are all equally "quadruple objects." Considered as fourfold—the iconic diagrammatic form—Harman's diagram can be read as both image and metaphor, referring back to its own ontology through the intermediary of itself, creating a hypoiconic feedback loop. Although Harman's diagram is thereby completed on its own terms, in the terms Harman uses to isolate and articulate space and time in relation to each other, the "diagram" here constitutes both background and foreground. Although Harman expresses his polarities through the bridge of a diagram possessing the visual authority, as Peirce would insist, of an "icon,"[70] Harman's diagram is both completely specific to him (how could it not be?) and diagrammatically multiversal, explicitly attempting to build bridges across universes. It is like the survivor's barrel in Poe's "A Descent into the Maelström," propelling him through the impossibly vast but utterly specific forces of nature.

Other scholars have argued with Harman's description of the degrees of finitude, or the number of poles and modes, but that is an angel-and-pin argument we can defer. As Lorraine Daston and Peter Galison's table of the evolution of the term objectivity shows,[71] there has never been a rational position not bounded by its historical context (fig. 44). Just as we cannot yet create an ontological diagram of nature, or history, we cannot easily create one of mental reality. What is significant is that his diagram, just one of the most recent in a five-millennia-long effort to reconcile the human gesture with the infinite possibilities of nature, is both fully complete and still open, achieving coherence without becoming the internally self-opposed table created by the other ardent diagrammaticists he cites, specifically Aristotle, Algirdas Julien Greimas, and Martin Heidegger. As with Tegmark's diagrammatic classifications of formal systems, this is not simply a disguised structural essentialism, pointing toward the kind of master narrative that poststructuralism sought to dismantle.

	1730 to present	1830 to present	1920 to present
Scientific Self	Sage	Worker	Expert
Image	Metaphysical	Mechanical	Interpreted
Practice	Intervention	Mechanical Transfer	Conditioned Judgment
Ontology	Universals	Individuals	Families

Fig. 44. Daston and Galison's overview of historically "objective" selves, showing how the "rational" position changes over time.

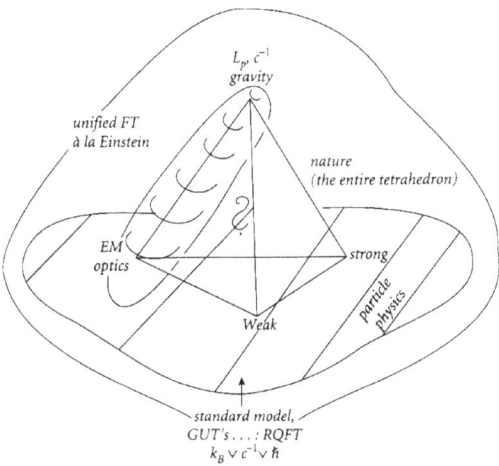

Fig. 45. Fröhlich's diagram of "nature."

Jürg Fröhlich's diagram of "nature" shows how the four basic forces, the strong and the weak, gravity and electromagnetism, can also be represented by a diagram (fig. 45). Exactly how they are able to exist in and affect the same universe at such massively distinct scales using so few basic particles and force carriers remains difficult for physics to explain, relying on a form of mathematical transformation called gauge symmetry to reconcile the actual invariance between such apparently diverse systems. The radical transformations required by gauge symmetry demonstrate that apparently nonhuman causal concepts cannot be easily or linearly universalized "subjectively" or "objectively," no matter how we define those terms. Attempting to simply reimpose universalized or enlarged versions of human subjectivity, deconstructivism, or even contemporary materialism—what Quentin Meillassoux has called "subjectalism"—is clearly an insufficient response. But so is any form of neorationalism, including Meillassoux's own.

Like Feynman and Barabási, Harman challenges the subjectively central position of human existence that has sustained the diagram for millennia. We do not yet have a shared language to describe changes in the intensity of our knowledge of ontological force relations (or tensions, junctions, and radiations, as Harman calls them), so we have no way to gauge the effect that a radical reduction in noetic complexity might create. But what we can do is create assemblages inside this condition, a diagram of what we can relate to that produces its own distinct form of knowledge. Any practice that seeks to describe an overall "reality" in any way, no matter how general or obscure, grandiose or personalized, must also always describe a relationship between the supporting forces and the forces and objects that oppose it. Harman's diagram provides a critical step toward any articulation of such force relations by offering an inclusive topology to access regional ontologies that have been warped away from each other. Like Tegmark's infinite tree, the assertions of Harman's diagram reveal a beguiling confidence in the universal search for mutual association that reinforces the polypsychic orientation of the diagram project. Harman's diagram both proliferates toward and secedes tidally away from multiple meanings, conveying us toward and through the totalizing hermeticism of real objects.

The last column of the last page of the edition of *The Temptation of the Diagram* includes Harman's diagram, along with several others that share this quality.

The recent discovery of the amplituhedron by Nima Arkani-Hamed is an example (fig. 46).[72] Just as Feynman replaced the pages of equations that came before his diagrammatic solution, this remarkable jewel-like form replaces the need for hundreds of Feynman diagrams with a single graphic equation. These diagrams point us to a radical reordering of our understanding of the basic materials of the physical universe, taking us further out, and deeper in, back once again to the ever more weirdly real. The role of the diagram as a divinatory device, as an infinity machine, still has a role to play.

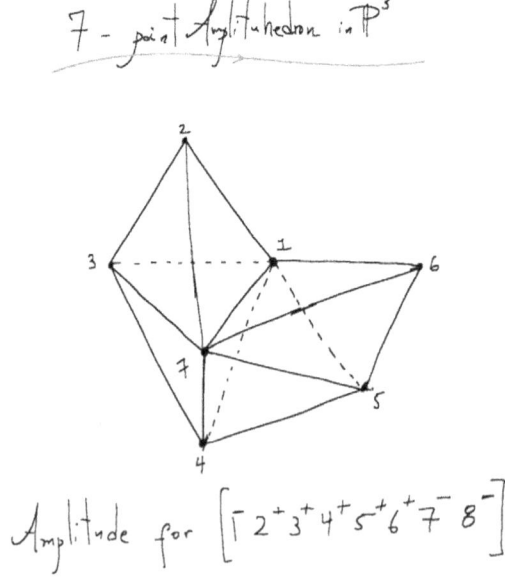

Fig. 46. A sketch of Arkani-Hamed's amplituhedron. Using Feynman diagrams, the same calculation would take roughly five hundred pages of algebra.

XVII
The degree to which we need speculation corresponds to the intensity of the novelty we are confronted with.
—Patrice Maniglier, "The Metaphysical Turn," 2015 [73]

Extending this idea of diagrammatic liberty into newly embodied and disembodied corporeal, political, environmental, and chronological relations may be necessary to allow us access to a newly existential "moment" that is equivalent, or even surpasses that confronting the original existentialists almost a century ago. The American Association for the Advancement of Science has recently published a study showing we have definitively, even defiantly, crossed four of the nine planetwide environmental boundaries within which humanity can safely operate.[74] The planetary boundary diagram provides a comprehensive overview of the oncoming Anthropocenic apocalypse, combining the strategies of divination with random walks (fig. 47).

And, like the thin line on the horizon that prefigures a tsunami, it is a signature of such nonlinear systems that they accelerate, engulfing their participant elements and entities, which are unaware of the true danger. Indeed, one need only to consider any human initiative to realize how much our models of the universe have been increasingly mathematized, our neurology quantized, our biochemistry molecularized, our attention medicated, our environment atomized, our food supply plasticized, and our economy globalized, to grasp how nature is becoming history, effectively inverting Roland Barthes's famous warning at the dawn of semiotics.[75]

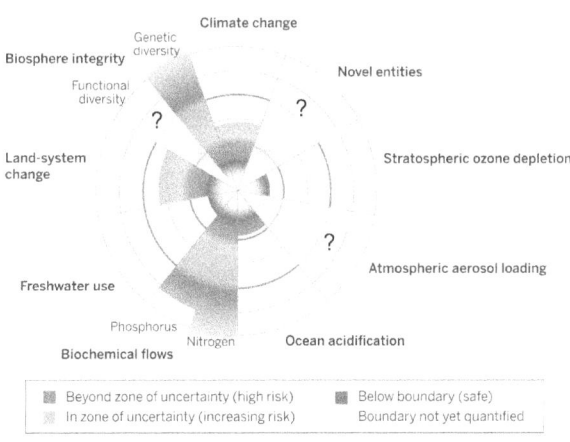

Fig. 47. The planetary boundary diagram combines the diagrammatic strategies of divination with Perrin's random walk and provides a comprehensive view of the oncoming Anthropocenic apocalypse.

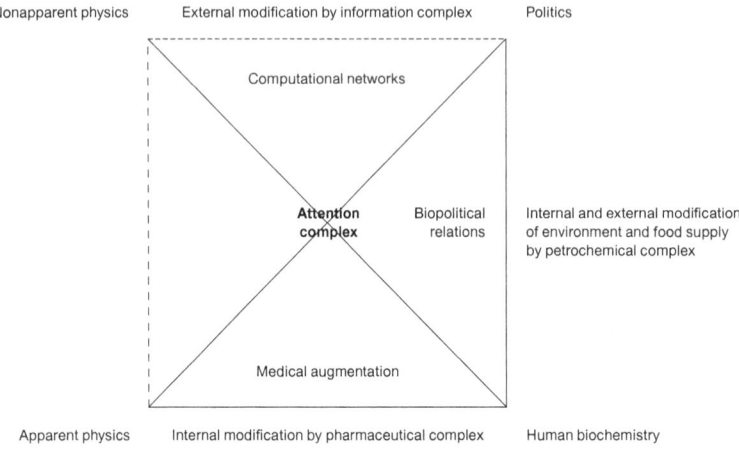

Fig. 48. Reciprocal human-to-object relations in the Anthropocene.

Having now established that at least some of the many diagrammatic systems referred to earlier in the essay are sympathetic to each other, perhaps we can usefully define some elements of this moment in four emergent complexes that together offer a suggestive view of contemporary and future human-nonhuman (or object-to-object) relations and provide a divinatory diagram for the present age (fig. 48).

The first complex—the transnational regime of petrochemical extraction and chief engine of the Anthropocene (indicated on the right side of the diagram)—finally achieved the dual status of both artificial nature and existential threat with the creation in the past century of the ozone hole. Its appetite and increasingly evident effects are by now widely known. The second, the information complex, described earlier and indicated in the top section, is the fusion of seven billion human Internet users and twelve billion machine operators (the emerging Internet of things), the offspring of Llull's *Ars Magna* and Swift's "Engine," which is quickly becoming an omnipresent cognitive partnership.

Combining with this system is a third, indicated on the lower section: the medical-industrial complex, which imports the effects and affects of the first and second complexes directly into the human body through psychopharmaceuticals, cybernetic organs, and so on, consistently exciting and degrading the human-to-nonhuman biological relations each person naturally supports, producing what Kenneth Rogers has called "the attention complex."

Finally, in a relentless exploratory process that shows no signs of exhaustion, all three human/nonhuman complexes are constantly stimulated by a fourth, shown on the left side of the diagram: the series of nonapparent scientific discoveries that have destabilized all notions of physical limits on scales at once astronomical, planetary, biological, and atomic. It is here that the distinction made earlier, between the web or network and its symbolic content becomes especially relevant. Although the human-oriented aspect of the network may be a driver of informational homogeneity, its object-oriented inclination to distribute new informational content from the exotic devices that we use to explore the universe is an unexpected source of informational diversity and renewed access to the "abductive." Although all complex systems must become more self-similar over time under the laws of thermodynamics, under the laws of quantum mechanics they can, and have, already developed into new and entirely unfamiliar states in other regions and scales of the universe. Radio telescopes regularly produce intermediated images of physics regimes and exotic particle interactions taking place at distances in space-time that dwarf all human existence. This "super-nature"—the intangible, invisible, nonapparent physics regime revealed within these experiments—seems consistent only in how arbitrary it is in human terms, reinforcing an overall sense of a universally contingent *kaos*, not an ordered *kosmos*. Chaotic systems of the kind discussed earlier are prone to such topological mixing, evolving over time so that any open region will eventually overlap with every other region. Although scientists may sometimes describe the universe as "decoherent," this is only to distinguish it from its original state of total quantum coherence. It does not mean the universe is ever "incoherent," although it may appear so to us. Once again, the collective strangeness of the physical world, multiplied over time, begins to outpace our wildest expectations and our ability to think the as-yet unthought. While in 1923 Nikos Kazantzakis could still plausibly imagine that, "We come from a dark abyss, we end in a dark abyss, and we call the luminous interval life,"[76] that epochal sense of an all-embracing universal darkness, which so characterized the original existentialism, has been replaced by the equally epic sensation that we are engulfed in a luminous ocean of possibilities. The universe is an infinitely radiant abyss, eternally emitting information on every frequency.

Exotic states such as the Bose-Einstein condensate and other recently discovered esoteric forms of quantum superposition may be only the beginning. Scientists have successfully demonstrated the reality of the previously hypothetical "dark matter," which constitutes 95 percent of the universe; has changed information into energy and back; changed light into matter and back; achieved quantum teleportation and neural telepathy; confirmed the existence of the Higgs boson or "God particle"; and, most recently, grown a human brain in a laboratory.

If Feynman, Frölich, and Arkani-Hamed hoped to reduce complexity and increase accessibility through their diagrams, during just the last few years scientific research has so many extraordinary advances that it seems to challenge our basic concepts of the possible.[77] Fed by satellites and distributed by the same Internet that produces informational homogeneity, computer-generated visions of multiple dimensions, chaotic states, and topological complexity produce radical alterity in both positive and negative scales, reinforcing our own decreasing direct proprioceptive access to universality. Figure 49, a diagram of the landscape of contemporary cosmology, references theoretical constructs such as M-Theory, the Holographic Principle, and Multiverse theory that would each require their own model of dimensionality to be perceptible. In a development that might have intrigued Duchamp and justified Lovecraft, the Holographic Principle proposes that our universe is indeed a kind of picture, produced and supported by multiple higher and lower dimensions. Contemporary scientific exploration requires such a comprehensive reordering of our proprioceptive limits that we will need to reset our perceptual frameworks at every level. Nonetheless, such diagrammatics are increasingly essential to examining a weirder perimeter of being that recognizes the limits of our cognitive framework, readmits the presence of new forces, and excites us to reimagine the potential role art may play in whatever form of society may emerge from these conditions.

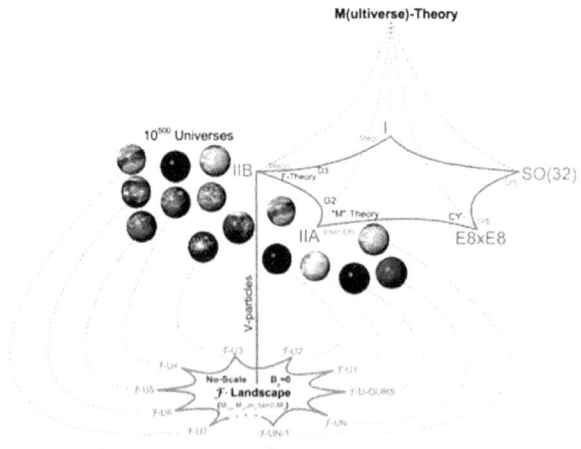

Fig. 49. The landscape of contemporary cosmology.

XVIII

These new and interconnected models of nature have already surpassed any human concepts of association, system or spectacle, and the consequent radical increase in nonlinear possibilities for any future definition of humanity must lead us to an equally radical shift in human thinking. Ignoring the full dimensions of this would be to ignore the need to restate the terms of human-to-human relations in transhuman ethical and political terms.

Figure 50 shows just some of the terms of traversal proposed by multiple thinkers. What quickly seems to emerge is an inherent tension between the terms used by various thinkers to universalize their agendas and the possibilities of human agency within those terms. If the opportunity is to create new approaches to transhuman potentials, the risk, which is one of relationality, not representation, is whether we must forgo any valuable aspects of our humanity to do so. Any materially grounded "ethics of seeing" raises questions of graduated value relations that are possibly inherent to materialism which seem especially complex.

Following the general policy of diagrammatic or eidetic severance has allowed tens of millions of stateless humans to be consigned to the limbo of partialized humanity that Giorgio Agamben calls *Homo Sacer*, with the planetary system that sustains us fast becoming a *Terra Sacra*, or cursed earth. The terms and conditions of the emergent intermediacy between new and newly recognizable nonhuman conditions need to be renegotiated. We may require a third legal system (one already being pursued in one form under the new crime of ecocide) that states clearly the ethics of the indeterminate middle ground between human "ownership," life,

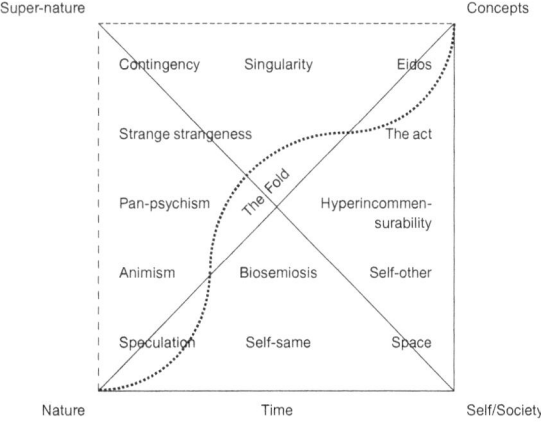

Fig. 50. Some philosophical propositions for reciprocal human-to-object relations in the Anthropocene.

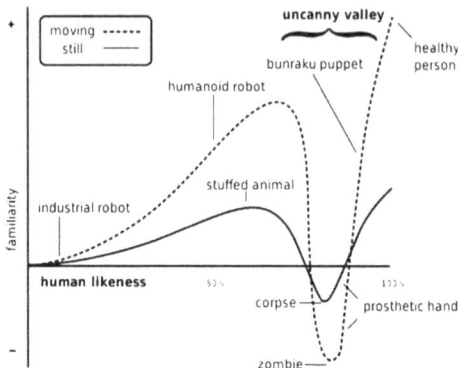

Fig. 51. Mori's "uncanny valley" proposes that a kind of vertical disassociation is inherent to nonhuman representation.

and otherwise self-sustaining systems. Even acknowledging the parallel existence of multiple *Homo Sacers*, like genetic deviations from genetic orthodoxy, or "wellness," is anathema to the current orthodoxies of bio-morality. Facing the emergence of new biotopes, the panicked burghers of the oikumene argue for biopolitical purity, even as the recently discovered CRISPR/Cas9 gene tool allows human DNA to be directly edited, potentially altering the genomes of entire populations. "We must be able to assume," perorates Jürgen Habermas, adopting the exclusionary voice of *Homo Civile*, "that we act and judge in *propria persona*—that it is our own voice speaking and no other."[78] That quasi-objects, hyperobjects, emitting knowledge networks, augmented perceptual systems, life-enhancing and life-degrading molecules, climactic systems, and bacterial flora are all now somehow "speaking," compels us to observe that Hume's bimodal logic of social justice will no longer be applicable to any emerging polity. A diagram that includes them is the necessary precursor to any dialogue with them. In the 1970s, the "uncanny valley" proposed by roboticist Masahiro Mori[79] illustrated the cognitive discomfort that suddenly appears when we encounter things that are unnervingly close to human, but not quite close enough, like robots, corpses, or "living" dolls (fig. 51).

Futurist Jamais Cascio has doubled down on Mori's diagram and proposed a way to envision this shift using the form of a second, or mirror, "uncanny valley" (fig. 52).[80] Wondering whether the physical presence, or absence, of emergent transhumans, networks, and biotopes will produce their own uncanny valley—challenging our own ability to intellectually accept the citizenship of possible new modes of being. Not everything will be as user-friendly as Scarlett Johansson's portrayal of the operating system calling itself "Samantha" in *Her*. Some of these systems may appear awkwardly alien, even demonic, to conventional human identity tropes. But as more and more "things" become parts of

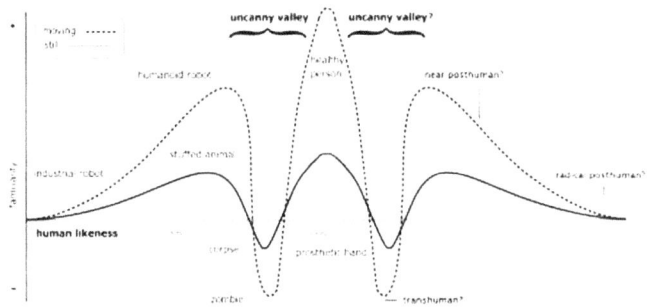

Fig. 52. Cascio's doubled uncanny valley imagines that the disassociation is redoubled for transhuman relations.

"people"—as networks become polities, as our informational ecosystem becomes richer—our imagination will be required to admit new and newly embodied forms of thinking, seeing, and speech.

In this vein, researcher Denise Herzing has recently proposed a tool for describing other types of intelligence called COMPLEX (Complexity of Markers for Profiling Life in Exobiology), which measures and scores five modes of complex behavioral response found in machines, dolphins, octopi, and microbes, as well as humans, suggesting that cognitive traits are not conditional on language production (fig. 53).[81]

Given sufficient scope in time and space, perhaps a new path integral, an outer limit, can be deduced. This integral will come to define whatever we choose to accept, or solicit, as "ourselves." This might even be what Emily Apter calls "something that solicits modes of being that exceed or bypass the hermeneutics of reading"[82] between knowledge and representation. When Cascio's second valley is laid over Herzing's

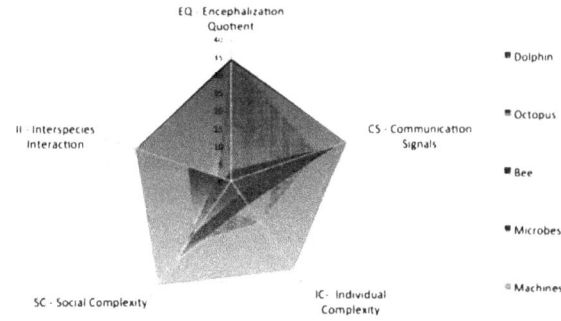

Fig. 53. Denise Herzing has recently proposed a tool for describing other types of intelligence, suggesting that cognitive traits are not conditional on language production.

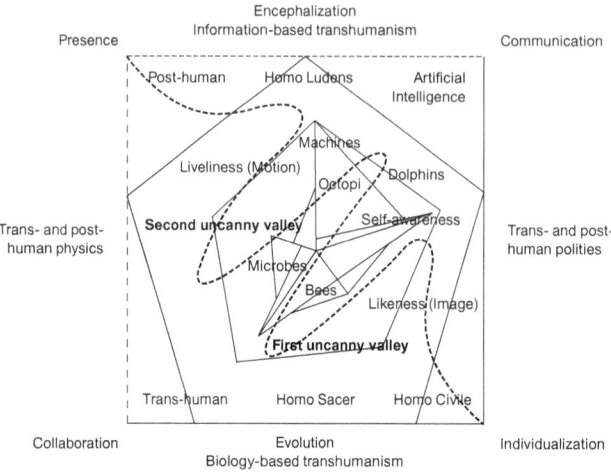

Fig. 54. When Cascio's second uncanny valley is laid over Herzing's diagram, we begin to see intercommunicative complexities emerge.

diagram (fig. 54), we begin to see new terms of exchange, an overlap of interspecies' intercommunicative states, premised against Herzing's prototype of a cognitive gauge symmetry.

This premise of coherent yet discrete realities, an intermodal topology of ontology, overlaps with the intercommunicative premise of both Herzing's and Harman's diagrams. As the century of the mirror-self evaporates, we will need to speak, and be spoken to, in languages other than our own. Revaluing existing communities using all five of Herzing's quotients creates a new and nonhierarchical space that could potentially be occupied by Johan Huizinga's *Homo Ludens*, a hypothetical future human for whom play and risk become integral forms of sociocultural participation. Our existing affinities with largely nonhuman systems, such as communication networks, farming collectives, adaptive epigenetics, stock markets, rapid transportation systems, recreational drugs, and online gaming systems, already foster complex interdependencies. It is perhaps not surprising that many of our representations of manifestations of extra-human transactional systems, or demons, involve contracts and gambling. Under the conditions that are emerging, increased biopolitical access to such a space could mean the emergence of new polities not limited by gender, class, or even species. If political power constitutes itself through relations between multiple forces, then Foucault's proposal that life must enter into history and form a "government of souls" can now be expanded to include all connected objects and systems, our larger "selves" distributed through multiple systems and modes of being, up to and including the expressive power of totalized planetary materiality, a vertiginous prospect for the existing models of biopolitical power.

XIX

As an artist, I'm most interested in the extent to which this environment, with its simultaneous advantages and problems, can be properly understood and utilized ethically, physically, and metaphysically as an exploratory tool. Insofar as the role of the artist remains experimental, an artist must explore, or be abducted, by the perimeter of being through the visualization of new bodies. Taken out of context, the trajectory of the art world network seemed entropically bound to a final condensation. But placed in the context of the preceding sequence of diagrams, with meaning being constructed by the participating viewer, subject to both negotiation and opposition on the part of the audience, with the identity of the viewer becoming more and more open to receiving information from a radiant and emitting universe, the essential openness of the diagrammatic approach introduces the possibility for the extension of art beyond local thermodynamic relations.

One possible way out is through the establishment of new symbolic axes and hubs, which in the case of art, means new genres. As Caroline Jones suggests in her own diagram of emergent artist types (fig. 55), there is no single answer, "no schema can capture the diversity in any present."[83]

If we are to face the hierarchy problem between our desire for intimacy and true universality, we will need to pursue something like an idea of a "cognitive gauge symmetry" that reconciles us to the difficulties and tensions of larger experience. Emerging spectra of cognitive traits, gender variance, identity, expression, and orientation already point to ways in which this might be manifested next, but also to ways in which the problem of disassociation within any diagrammatic ontology represents itself at every scale.

. **Immersive**   the "cave" paradigm, the virtual helmet, the black-box video, the earphone set
. **Alienated**   taking technology and "making it strange," exaggerating attributes to provoke shock, using technologies to switch senses or induce disorientation
. **Interrogative**   work that repurposes or remakes devices to enhance their insidious or wondrous properties; available data translated into sensible systems
. **Residual**   work that holds on to an earlier technology, repurposes or even fetishizes and abandoned one
. **Resistant**   work that refuses to use marketed technologies for their stated purpose; work that pushes viewers to reject technologies or subvert them
. **Adaptive**   work that takes up technologies and extends or applies them for creative purposes, producing new subjects for the technologies in question

Fig. 55. Jones's table of emerging artist types.

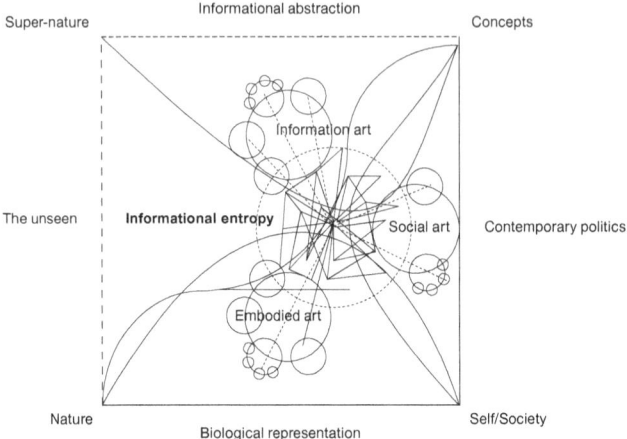

Fig. 56. While genres begin to overlap and condense, following the laws of thermodynamics, new genres are born through the introduction of new information systems.

But some of the new genres already being developed during the most recent phase shift can be specifically aligned to the axes of transhuman development shown in Figure 56. On the upper axis, the appearance of transhuman informational systems can be registered in forms of informational mediation, sometimes carried out through digital painting overlaid with remnants of expressionism. On the lower axis, the emergence of transhuman biological systems can be seen in newly embodied forms of biosocial identity, often propagated through video and Web art. On the left side, the emergence of new polities can be seen in works that comment on new forms of social structure, often performatively, in ways that reflect the economic or environmental disruption caused by anthropogenic change.

As the diagram implies, these genres often overlap, without looking too closely at how the specific formal terms of such an increasingly processed, intercommunicative, and networked world are determining their own basic conditions of inquiry and agency.

We return to Stjernfelt's admonition that, "Diagrammatical experimentation is . . . only made possible by gaining access to a landscape by means of a body."[84] Even limited to a planetary scale, the recognizance of our newly distributed selves will require both a physical and ethical rescaling and a reimagining of what we define as human. As fictional cosmonaut Kris Kelvin comes to painfully understand in the novel *Solaris* (1961), perhaps the Ur tale of our age, when faced with the unknown we are the ones who must choose whether to use science morally or immorally—and what those terms will allow us to include. Who knows how additional dimensions, categorical changes, or more complex topologies might affect our reading of questions of mutuality, force relations, relative isomorphism, folding, and disassociation in the future? We have arrived at another essentially diagrammatic moment, the impossibility of endings.

XX

While at the GRI, I developed two potential versions of this project. The first was an index of diagrams, a kind of diagram of diagrams, that anticipated the collection of historical diagrams that have been layered and accumulated in the edition, which, whether I call it an anti-history or not, has still become a kind of history of diagrams.

But objects, even diagrams, can only be viewed through their connections with other objects. To fully honor the central premise of this diagrammatic inquiry and the doubled nature of diagrams as both vector and table, the project must consistently reject the comfort of its own tabulatory instincts and open itself back up to connecting to future diagrams—and diagrams of such diagrams. In the spirit of such ardent speculation, the following series of my own diagrams continue this premise as a visual game for the reader. For the purposes of continuity, the fourfold is used as a template for this comparative exercise, although it remains to be seen if this archetypal diagrammatic form can yet serve as a useful skeleton for further speculation, or constrains it like an exoskeleton.

We must first establish that, potentially, all of the concepts discussed can be presented in a single isomorphic diagram. What is important is that fundamental topological relations are conserved but not confined by similarity and local isomorphisms. At a minimum we

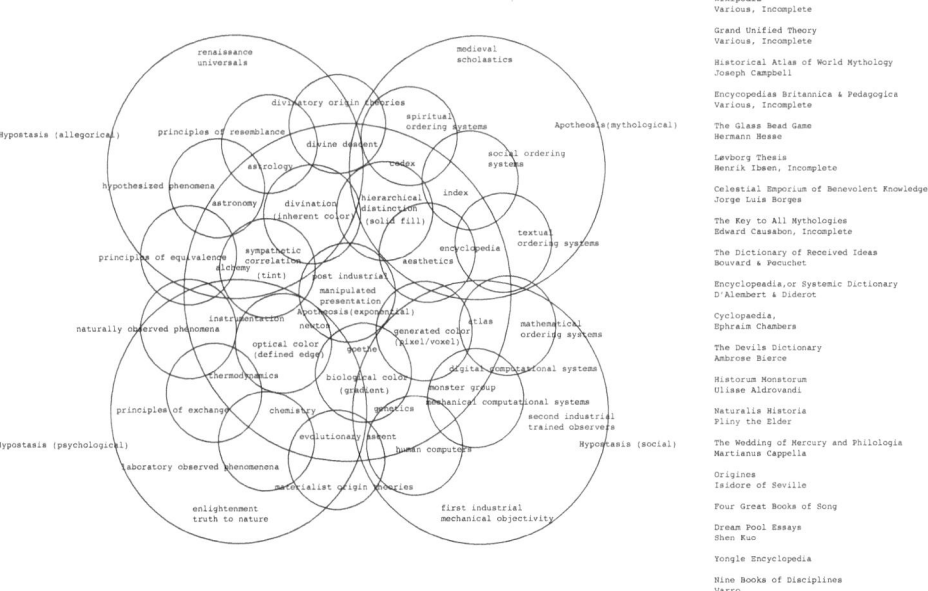

Fig. 57. Integrated historic visualization systems.

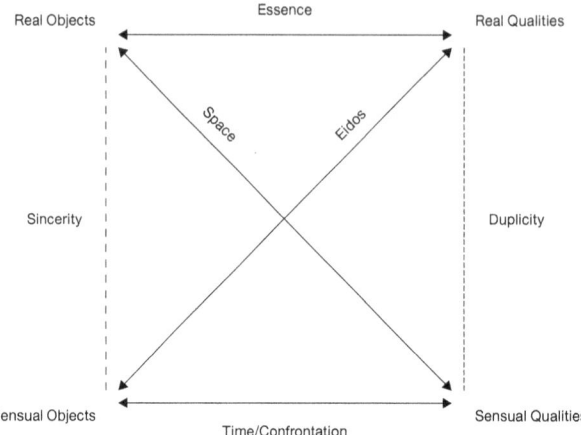

Fig. 58. Harman's diagram reduced to its basic relations.

should include the three diagrams explicitly mentioned at the start of this essay, Harman's quadruple object, Peirce's theory of semiotics, and Husserl's time diagrams. We will begin with a simplified form of Harman's fourfold diagram (figs. 58–60).

Oriented to Harman's diagram, Peirce's semiotic triangle can now also be rotated to occupy the right lower half of the square, and his concept of eidetic "abduction," or guesswork, can also be placed firmly along the same axis.

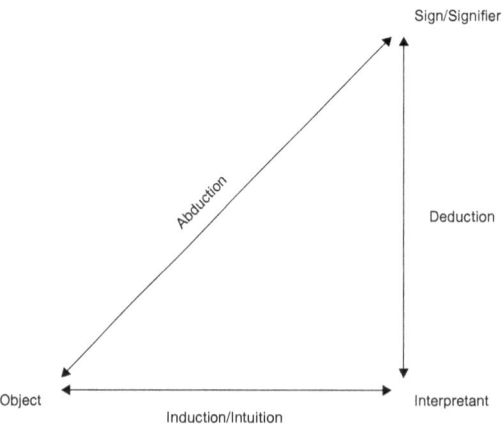

Fig. 59. Peirce's semiotic triangle reoriented to match Harman's square. The axis of abduction orients us toward what we do not know.

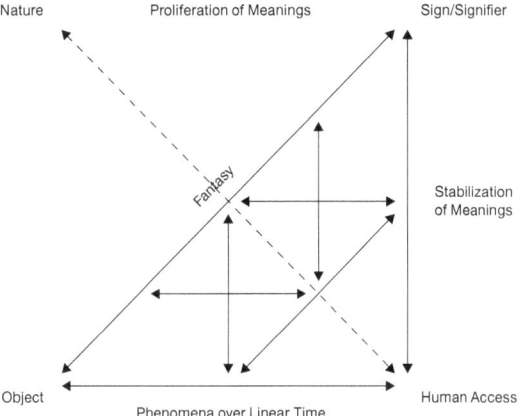

Fig. 60. Husserl's diagram reoriented to match Harman's square. The axis of fantasy orients us toward what we have not experienced.

Earlier in this essay, I briefly referenced Husserl's theory of experienced time and its concept of "noema" as being essential to both Harman and Stjernfelt. Husserl used descriptive psychology and logic to propose an eidetic science of consciousness, a geometry of experience, examining the poetic potential for examining the abyssal nature of time, a direct inspiration for the existentialists, through what Husserl called fantasy, or the ability to discern alternatives to reality. Husserl's concept of fantasy, or the ability to discern alternatives to reality. Husserl's concept of fantasy can be placed firmly along the axis of what Harman calls "eidos" and Peirce calls "abduction."

Harman's diagram of how we experience everything is now linked with Peirce's semiotic model of how we experience objects, and Husserl's model of how we experience time. So far, so good. But Harman's, Peirce's, and Husserl's diagrams are all cut from the same cloth, neatly dividing space, perception, and time into discrete quadrants. One of the most difficult problems faced by science and art remains a bias toward the literal representation of tensed time inherent to the diagram. The question of the contingent imagination, raised by David Hume and diagrammed by Peirce as the abductive axis, remains open. Francisco Varela's anticipatory theory and diagram of time proposed the concept of "protention" to complement memory or "retention" and at least give a name to our ability to anticipate any eidetic variation in advance of our own direct experience of it. We are not only dealing with human concepts of causality. It is very likely that consciousness is a partially quantum-based multiphasic process and enjoys more, and more complex, relative degrees of freedom within the subjective moment and the fixed structure of chronological or block time than Ockham could

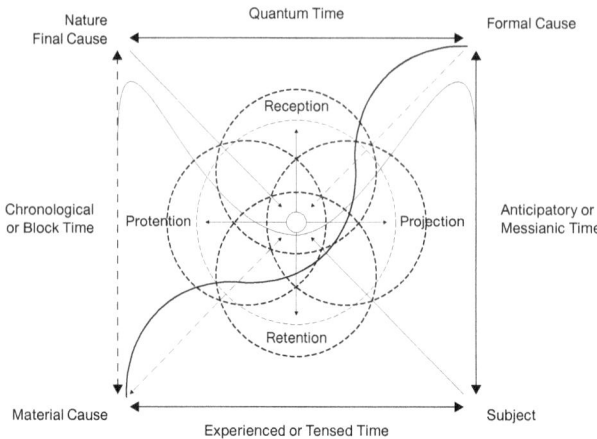

Fig. 61. Four axes of time. Our lived experience, including the concept of free will, is conducted along one axis, paralleled by quantum events, while the eschatological process of messianic time unfolds along the parallel axis of chronological or fixed time.

imagine. We will need to add one more form of time, quantum time, to the threefold model of time developed earlier in Figure 6.

We might further propose two more terms to complement Varela's ideas of "protention" and "retention." The space between the infinite hopes of predication and the compromised reality of predictability already occupy a significant part of our mental structure. "Reception" seems a suitable term to describe how we accept and accommodate the quantum effects that we cannot yet measure or register and "projection" seems useful to reflect the deep-seated human need to project our hopes and desires into the future, a kind of eudaimonic imagination. Even taken together, the four forms of time and the four modes of human participation in Figure 61 are still a form of Molina's Middle Knowledge, concerned with the projection of the human perception of time onto the universe. We cannot simply ignore those manifestations of space and time that can in some circumstances even be curved, slowed, or even run backward. We need to add a diagram of the spatial constructs and unseen force hierarchies that are occupying and distorting Einstein's much larger space-time, affecting any human reception of such radiative intensity.

In Figure 62 we can see that as any world line travels through space-time, it must experience radical flux as space and time rotate and warp its passage, with each side of the graph registering its passage in a temporally distinct form and participating in their own external force relations. In place of the earlier rigid geometry of space-time, a quadruply warped surface creates pockets and peaks of experience, while still maintaining a topologically invariant surface, "our" space and time, indicated by the bold lines, becomes a force amplifier for what Harman calls vertical disassociation.

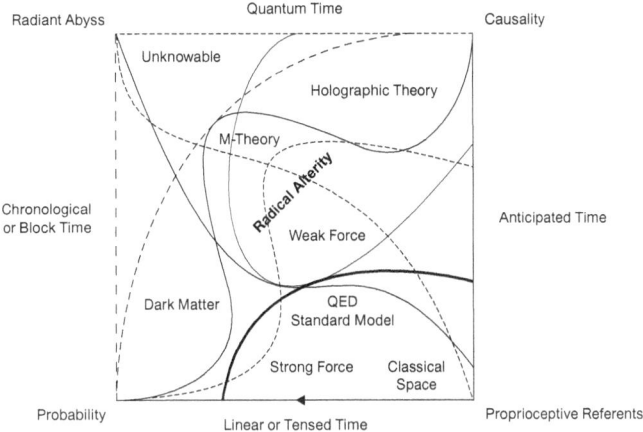

Fig. 62. All axes are distorted by unseen force hierarchies occupying and distorting space-time.

In a contemporary echo of Laplace's "Intellect," Seth Lloyd at MIT has calculated that a total of 10^{120} elementary operations have been performed on 10^{90} bits of information, the number of bits in the universe.[85] But although we are now able to count the "bits" of information in the universe and the number of operations they might undergo, we cannot visualize them. While contemporary mathematical solutions are being developed to visualize multiple path integrals that can follow such superposed curvature in quantum space and time but for the moment, to accurately diagram even a single space-time path, or world line, in this space is impossible. It would become intertwined with itself, chaotically twisted around its own past world lines by the relative spin of the space-time continuum, a billion Lorenz butterflies scattering in a Lévy flight. While it is still impossible to visualize these traces, can our much simpler mash-up of Aristotle, Harman, Barabási, Husserl, Herzing, Einstein, and Peirce coexist with this model of space-time? Let's give it a shot, after all, we may just need a couple more diagrams.

In the polyverse proposed here, "only connect" becomes a mandate, as intercommunicative polymodal gradients dramatically alter our experience of the complexity of a conceptual space. It has been established that information and material are equivalent. This implies some potential for a theory of potentially unifying cognitive gauge symmetries in multidimensional space. As shown, the space-time continuum is physically warped by at least three complementary modes of time and only then humanly interpreted by a fourth. In the immediate present the four forms of time (that we are currently aware of) register flux on so many levels that our inability to decode that process renders it apparently incomprehensible.

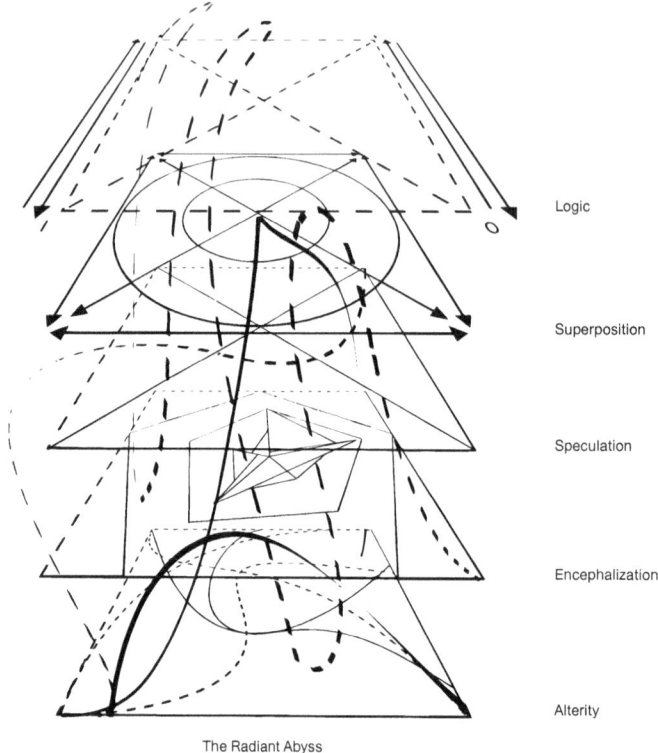

Fig. 63. As any concept travels through space-time creating its unique world line, elements of the preceding diagrammatic approaches register and distort its passage in distinct but superposed forms.

But in the long term, our ability to propose new and inclusive models is unlimited. By this measure, informational evolution is a nonlinear series of imaginative and temporal opportunities, whose program is the eventual but nonsimultaneous occupation of every spectrum of the space-time continuum, from which also emerges the coextensive acceptance of consequential and ongoing change. This produces a forcible reengagement with what Emmanuel Levinas called "deep time": the producer of true alterity. Figure 63 shows how elements of the preceding diagrams, which could be shuffled like a deck of cards, might begin to collectively register and affect concepts like logic, speculation, alterity and encephalization in their distinct but superposed forms. Taking this concept further, we might even begin to propose a viable ethics of seeing that are dependent on plural relations, and by extension, a politics of diagrammatic thinking. The signal virtues of the diagram as an exploratory tool for exploring this polyverse have hopefully been conclusively demonstrated here. Perhaps the difference between an abyss and a slope can finally be understood as one of moving across gradients, instead of between categories.

By examining the passive and active terms of the imagination through diagrams, which is what also seems to be going on here, perhaps we can now also begin to collectively articulate an anticipatory and projective transhuman art, based both on what is embedded in the world and on that which is oriented toward an ethical politics of the future. Imagination is a form of information embedded in the future, often mixing protention and projection. A diagram of diagrams should allow us infinite space to shape the unknown, to mouth the unsayable word, to glimpse the unseeable object from the corner of our eye, to gesture toward the truly unthinkable.

In choosing between the kinds of nonlinear behaviors that artists could mimic from artificial nature, we cannot yet easily see the difference between exotic approaches such as chaos, multistability, aperiodic oscillation, and amplitude death, but perhaps we don't have to. One characteristic of an art that could address this state might be its active cultivation of the sense that something is emerging other than the artist and the viewer, an anticipation of informational and material possibilities embedded unpredictably in, and through, interconnected objects in space and time that hold the work open—"or, more precisely, maintain the work as this opening."[86] This emergent form may initially seem impenetrable to any immediate reading from the human perspective, too large to understand or too detailed to grasp in a moment , But if we abandon our framing structure and collapse Figure 63 into itself, a body begins to be revealed (fig. 64). The demon, free at last.

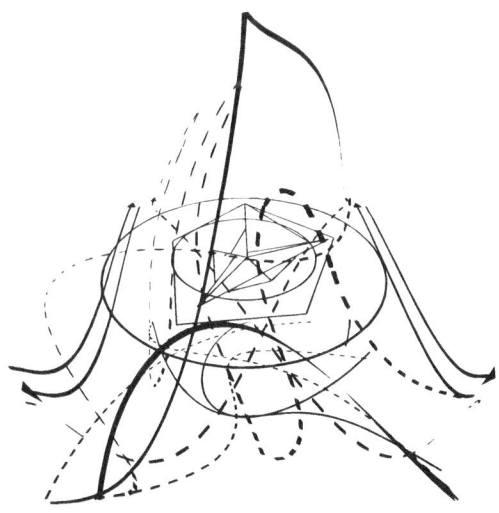

Fig. 64. If we abandon the framing structures of Figure 63, a body begins to emerge.

Artists may need to become such figures to survive and flourish, becoming closer to the self-reinforcing solitary waves called solitons, arrows in an infinite field, arcing all the way forward, up, in, between, and out—or at least as far as the ontological structure of the universe will allow us. A new kind of demon for a new kind of diagram. A creature of the radiant abyss, as much information as material.

Outpacing the new nature—the synthesis of physics, biology, and chemistry that defines that perimeter—will require a new kind of anthropology, an embrace of contingency beyond anything we have yet known or expressed. The only way to communicate may be through the language of rapidly evolving systems, to coerce, copulate, collaborate, and corrupt—all things that diagrams do exceptionally well—cultivating an ethics of seeing based on inclusion and intermodality, and a politics of thinking based on continuous reconnection. Such interpositionality is not a form of surrender to doubt, or the oppressive inevitability of chance but a doubling-down on the repotentialization of possibility. It will be strange. It should be strange. In this game, the winner is the player that increases the possibilities for all.

We are in this, by which I mean everything, all the way, together. In other words, it's your turn to move beyond words, to continue the game, the conversation, the diagram.[87] Imagine a single dimension, a point. Add a line. Now add an arrow to the line, a vector. Can you imagine another dimension? Go ahead. Add another line, another, and another. Now add arrows to all those lines. More!

ACKNOWLEDGMENTS

I am profoundly indebted to everyone at the Getty Research Institute, Columbia University, the Mellon Foundation, the Andrea Rosen Gallery, and especially David Brafman, Gail Feigenbaum, Rachel Furnari, Natilee Harren, Daisy Nam, Amy Ontiveros, Marcia Reed, and Andrea Rosen for supporting my interest in this entire area of research. My thanks to Michele Ciaccio and Jenelle Porter for their thoughtful editing.

Albert-László Barabási, Bettina Funcke, Caroline Jones, Graham Harman, Kenneth Rogers, and Frederik Stjernfelt all participated in series of colloquia at Columbia University in 2013 titled "A Time for Everything: The Temptation of the Diagram," where many of these ideas were developed. I remain enthralled by their insights. The colloquia were generously supported by the Mellon Foundation.

Portions of this essay were separately published in *Retracing the Expanded Field: Encounters between Art and Architecture*, ed. Spyros Papapetros and Julian Rose (Cambridge, MA: MIT Press, 2014); *Realism, Materialism, Art*, edited by Christoph Cox, Jenny Jaskey, and Suhail Malik (Annandale-on-Hudson, NY: The Center for Curatorial Studies, Bard College, Sternberg Press, 2015); *The New Existentialism*, edited by Tim Griffin (The Kitchen, forthcoming) and *October* 155 (Spring 2016). I am deeply grateful to the editors for their patience and forbearance.

NOTES

1. Gustave Flaubert, *The Temptation of Saint Anthony*, trans. Lafcadio Hearn (New York: Modern Library, 2001), 179.
2. Susanne Leeb, *A Line with Variable Direction, Which Traces No Contour and Delimits No Form, Drawing a Hypothesis* (Heidelberg: Springer, 2011), 33.
3. Patricia Falguières, *134 Views of the World, Urgent Painting* (Paris: Musée d'Art Moderne de la Ville de Paris, 2002), 28.
4. See pp. 22–23, 140–41.
5. Isabelle Graw, *Thinking through Painting* (Berlin: Sternberg Press, 2012), 57.
6. Geoffrey Sampson, *Writing Systems: A Linguistic Introduction* (Stanford, CA: Stanford University Press, 1985), 32.
7. Reviel Netz, *The Shaping of Deduction in Greek Mathematics: A Study in Cognitive History* (Cambridge: Cambridge University Press, 2003), 37.
8. Bruno Latour and Adam Lowe, "The Migration of the Aura—Exploring the Original through Its Facsimiles," in *Switching Codes*, ed. Thomas Bartscherer and Roderick Coover (Chicago: University of Chicago Press, 2010).
9. Aristotle, *On Interpretation*, trans. Harold P. Cooke (Cambridge, MA: Harvard University Press, 1938).
10. William of Ockham, *Tractatus de praedestinatione et de futuris contingentibus* (London: Hackett, 1983).
11. Samuel Y. Edgerton, Jr., *The Renaissance Rediscovery of Linear Perspective* (New York: Harper & Row, 1975), 161.
12. Edgerton, *The Renaissance Rediscovery*, 163.
13. Peter Øhrstrøm, "What William of Ockham and Luis de Molina Would Have Said to Nuel Belnap: A Discussion of Some Arguments against 'The Thin Red Line,'" in *Nuel Belnap on Indeterminism and Free Action*, ed. Thomas Müller (New York: Springer, 2014), 175.
14. Krzysztof Pomian, "Vision and Cognition," in *Picturing Science, Producing Art*, ed. Caroline Jones and Peter Galison (London: Routledge, 1998), 228.
15. Michel Foucault, *The Order of Things: An Archaeology of the Human Sciences* (New York: Pantheon Books, 1971), 201.
16. Alexander Pope, Introduction to his translation of Homer's *Odyssey*, (London: Printed for Henry Lintot, 1725).
17. Pierre Simon Laplace, *A Philosophical Essay on Probabilities*, trans. F. L. Emory and F. W. Truscott (New York: Dover, 1951), 4.
18. Edwin John Ellis and William Butler Yeats, eds., *The Works of William Blake; Poetic, Symbolic, and Critical* (London: B. Quaritch, 1893), vol. 1, 250.
19. Edgar Allan Poe, "A Descent into the Maelström," in Thomas O. Mabbott, ed., *The Collected Works of Edgar Allan Poe—Vol. II: Tales and Sketches* (Cambridge: The MIT Press, 1978), 574–97. The epigraph is from Joseph Glanvill, "Against Confidence in Philosophy, and Matters of Speculation," in idem, *Essays on Several Important Subjects in Philosophy and Religion* (London: Printed by J.D. for John Baker . . . and Henry Mortlock . . . , 1676), 15: "The ways of God in *Nature* (as in *Providence*) are not as ours are: Nor are the models that we frame any way commensurate to the vastness and profundity of His works; which have a *depth* in them greater than the *Well* of *Democritus*."
20. Edgar Allan Poe, "The Philosophy of Composition," *Graham's Magazine* 28, no. 4 (April 1846): 163.
21. Edgar Allan Poe, *Eureka, A Prose Poem* (New York: Putnam, 1848).
22. Poe, *Eureka*, 50.

23. Charles Sanders Peirce, *Collected Papers of C. S. Peirce*, ed. C. Hartshorne, P. Weiss, and A. Burks (Cambridge, MA: Harvard University Press, 1931–58), vol. 2, 228. "A sign, or *representamen*, is something which stands to somebody for something in some respect or capacity. It addresses somebody, that is, creates in the mind of that person an equivalent sign, or perhaps a more developed sign. That sign which it creates I call the *interpretant* of the first sign. The sign stands for something, its *object* [or referent]. It stands for that object, not in all respects, but in reference to a sort of idea, which I have sometimes called the *ground* of the representamen."
24. Quentin Meillassoux, *The Number and The Siren: A Decipherment of Mallarmé's "Coup de dés,"* trans. Robin Mackay (London: Urbanomic, 2012), 221.
25. Stephane Mallarmé, *Crise de Vers*, in Rosemary Lloyd, *Mallarmé: The Poet and His Circle* (New York: Cornell University Press, 2005), 231.
26. J. N. Mohanty, *Edmund Husserl's Freiburg Years, 1916–1938* (New Haven: Yale University Press, 2011), 21, 69.
27. J. W. Gibbs, Part 1, "Graphical Methods in the Thermodynamics of Fluids" and Part 2, "A Method of Geometrical Representation of the Thermodynamic Properties of Substances by Means of Surfaces," (Transactions of the Connecticut Academy, Vol. II, 1873), Part 1, 309, Part 2, 383.
28. Karl Pearson, "The Problem of the Random Walk," *Nature* 72 (1905): nos. 1865 (p. 294); 1866 (p. 318); 1867 (p. 342).
29. Paul Klee, *Pedagogical Sketchbook*, trans. Sibyl Moholy-Nagy (London: Faber & Faber, 1953), 54. Figure 30 appears on page 35.
30. Wassily Kandinsky, *Concerning the Spiritual in Art*, trans. M. T. H. Sadler (New York: Dover, 1977), 6.
31. Kazimir Malevich, *The Non-Objective World: The Manifesto of Suprematism*, trans. Howard Dearstyne (Mineola, NY: Dover, 2003), 51.
32. Klee, *Pedagogical Sketchbook*, 61.
33. Hannes Meyer, 1928; as quoted by Theo van Leeuwen, *Introducing Social Semiotics* (New York: Routledge, 2005), 71.
34. Jules Cotard, "Du délire hypocondriaque dans une forme grave de la mélancholie anxieuse," *Annales Médico-Psychologiques* 4 (1880): 168–74.
35. Linda Dalrymple Henderson, *Duchamp in Context: Science and Technology in the Large Glass* (Princeton University Press, 1998), 32.
36. As comprehensively discussed in Linda Dalrymple Henderson, *The Fourth Dimension and Non-Euclidean Geometry in Modern Art* (Cambridge, MA: MIT Press, 1983).
37. As explored by David Joselit in "Dada's Diagrams," in Leah Dickerman and Matthew Witkovsky, eds., *The Dada Seminars* (New York: D.A.P., 2005), 221–39.
38. Joselit, "Dada's Diagrams," 34.
39. "This experiment [of the *Three Standard Stoppages*] was made in 1913 to imprison and preserve forms obtained through chance, through my chance." Marcel Duchamp, "Apropos of Myself," in Anne d'Harnoncourt and Kynaston McShine, eds., *Marcel Duchamp* (New York: Museum of Modern Art, 1973), 273.
40. Graham Harman, *Weird Realism: Lovecraft and Philosophy* (Arlesford: Zero Books, 2012).
41. Michel Houellebecq, *H. P. Lovecraft: Against the World against Life* (San Francisco: Believer Books, 2005), 64.
42. Houellebecq, *H. P. Lovecraft*, 75.
43. Houellebecq, *H. P. Lovecraft*, 79.
44. Donald Tyson, "Yog-Sothoth," in *The Gods of H. P. Lovecraft* (San Francisco: Journal Stone, 2015).
45. Reza Negarestani, *Cyclonopedia: Complicity with Anonymous Materials* (Melbourne: re.press, 2008), 199.
46. Negarestani, *Cyclonopedia*, 28.
47. Negarestani, *Cyclonopedia*, 43.
48. Manuel DeLanda, "Deleuze, Diagrams, and the Genesis of Form," *ANY: Architecture New York* 23 (June 1998): 30.
49. Max Tegmark, "The Multiverse Hierarchy," in Bernard Carr, ed., *Universe or Multiverse?* (Cambridge: Cambridge University Press, 2007), 117.
50. Gilles Deleuze, *Francis Bacon: The Logic of Sensation*, trans. Daniel W. Smith (New York: Continuum, 2003), 110.
51. Frederik Stjernfelt, *Diagrammatology: An Investigation on the Borderlines of Phenomenology, Ontology, and Semiotics* (Heidelberg: Springer, 2007), 306.
52. Stjernfelt, *Diagrammatology*, 290.
53. Stjernfelt, *Diagrammatology*, 159.
54. Allan Kaprow, "The Legacy of Jackson Pollock," *ARTnews* 57, no. 6 (1958): 26.
55. Brian O'Doherty, *American Masters: The Voice and the Myth* (New York: Random House, 1982), 106.
56. Gilles Deleuze and Felix Guattari, *A Thousand Plateaus: Capitalism and Schizophrenia*, trans. Brian Massumi (Minneapolis: University of Minnesota Press, 1987), 146.
57. See pp. 24–25. *The Temptation of the Diagram*, Andrea Rosen Gallery, New York, March 30–April 27, 2013. The exhibition featured Aranda\Lasch, Archigram, Matthew Barney, Joseph Beuys, Earle Brown,

Trisha Brown, Mel Bochner, John Bock, Lygia Clark, Max Ernst, Öyvind Fahlström, Thomas Hirschhorn, Steven Holl, Barry Le Va, Mark Lombardi, Thom Mayne, Julie Mehretu, Matt Mullican, Matthew Ritchie, Katy Schimert, Carolee Schneemann, Rudolf Steiner, Wolfgang Tillmans, and Bernar Venet, and was organized by Matthew Ritchie.

58. Mel Bochner, "Anyone Can Learn To Draw," press release for *Drawings*, Galerie Heiner Friedrich, Munich, 1969.

59. Bernice Rose and Ann Temkin, *Thinking Is Form: The Drawings of Joseph Beuys* (London: Thames & Hudson, 1993).

60. Gilles Deleuze, *Foucault*, trans. Séan Hand (Minneapolis: University of Minnesota Press, 1988), 44.

61. Rosalind Krauss, "Sculpture and the Expanded Field," *October* 8 (Spring 1979): 44.

62. Krauss, "Sculpture and the Expanded Field," 43.

63. That the definitive "follows" of the first and second sentence is succeeded by the weaker "seems" of the third sentence *seems* to be a tacit acknowledgment that Krauss's own aesthetic leanings might trump the inherent logic of the statement.

64. Sol LeWitt, "Sentences on Conceptual Art," in *0–9* (New York, 1969).

65. Bruno Latour, *We Have Never Been Modern*, trans. Catherine Porter (Cambridge, MA: Harvard University Press, 1993), Figure 3.3, 58.

66. Martijn P. van den Heuvel and Olaf Sporns, "Rich-Club Organization of the Human Connectome," *The Journal of Neuroscience* 31 (November 2011): 15775–86.

67. Shoichi Toyabe et al., "Experimental Demonstration of Information-to-Energy Conversion and Validation of the Generalized Jarzynski Equality," *Nature Physics* 6 (2010): 988–92.

68. In 1995, a team of scientists produced the first Bose-Einstein condensate, and other recently discovered exotic forms of quantum superposition have followed.

69. Hermann Hesse, *The Glass Bead Game*, trans. Richard and Clara Winston (1969); first published by Holt, Rinehart & Winston in 1943: "These rules, the sign language and grammar of the Game, constitute a kind of highly developed secret language drawing upon several sciences and arts, but especially mathematics and music (and/or musicology), and capable of expressing and establishing interrelationships between the content and conclusions of nearly all scholarly disciplines. The Glass Bead Game is thus a mode of playing with the total contents and values of our culture; it plays with them as, say, in the great age of the arts a painter might have played with the colours on his palette."

70. Graham Harman, *The Quadruple Object* (Arlesford: Zero Books, 2011), 79.

71. Lorraine Daston and Peter Galison, *Objectivity* (New York: Zone Books, 2007), 414.

72. Nima Arkani-Hamed et al., "Scattering Amplitudes and the Positive Grassmannian," *Journal of High Energy Physics* (December 2012): 8.

73. Patrice Maniglier, "The Metaphysical Turn: Reflections on 'Speculative Realism,'" in *The New Existentialism*, ed. Tim Griffin (New York: The Kitchen, forthcoming).

74. Will Steffen et al., "Planetary Boundaries: Guiding Human Development on a Changing Planet," *Science* 347, no. 6223 (February 13, 2015).

75. Roland Barthes, *Mythologies*, trans. Annette Lavers (New York: Noonday Press, 1972), prologue.

76. Nikos Kazantzakis, *The Saviors of God: Spiritual Exercises*, trans. Kimon Friar (New York: Simon & Schuster, 1923), prologue.

77. Ginestra Bianconi and Albert-László Barabási, "Bose-Einstein Condensation in Complex Networks," abstract, *Physical Review Letters* 86, no. 24 (2001): 5632–35.

78. Jurgen Habermas, *The Future of Human Nature* (Cambridge: Polity Press, in association with Blackwell, 2003), 57.

79. Masahiro Mori, "Bukimi No Tani" (The Uncanny Valley), *Energy* 7, no. 4 (1970): 33–35; published in English as "The Uncanny Valley," *Robotics & Automation Magazine* 19, no. 2 (2012): 98–100.

80. Jamais Cascio, "The Second Uncanny_Valley," www.openthefuture.com/2007/10/the_second_uncanny_valley.html.

81. Denise L. Herzing, "Profiling Nonhuman Intelligence: An Exercise in Developing Unbiased Tools for Describing Other Types of Intelligence on Earth," *Acta Astronautica* 94, no. 2 (2014): 676–80.

82. Emily Apter, "Preamble on Modes of Existence: Souriau, Latour and Stenghers," in *The New Existentialism*, ed. Tim Griffin (New York: The Kitchen, forthcoming).

83. Caroline A. Jones, *The Mediated Sensorium* (Cambridge, MA: MIT Press, 2006), 6.

84. Stjernfelt, *Diagrammatology*, 290.

85. Seth Lloyd, "Computational Capacity of the Universe," *Physical Review Letters* 88, no. 23 (2002): 237901.

86. Apter, "Preamble on Modes of Existence."

87. It was in this spirit that I developed both a third iteration of *The Temptation of the Diagram*, collecting all the diagrams I had worked with into two volumes and then a fourth iteration in 2014 that algorithmically abstracts the historical content found in the books and then enlarges it into a two-hundred-foot-long wallpaper, dissolving the illusory chronological distance between historically bound gesture and diagrammatic meaning, transforming it from image to environment. This version of the project presents the viewer with another question: at what scale does the diagram become reality?

ILLUSTRATION CREDITS

Figure 1. From Geoffrey Sampson, *Writing Systems: A Linguistic Introduction* (Stanford, CA: Stanford University Press, 1985), 32.
Figure 2. Matthew Ritchie, 2016.
Figure 3. From Bruno Latour and Adam Lowe, "The Migration of the Aura—Exploring the Original Through Its Facsimiles," in *Switching Codes*, ed. Thomas Bartscherer (Chicago: University of Chicago Press, 2010).
Figure 4. Matthew Ritchie, 2016.
Figure 5. From Peter Øhrstrøm, "What William of Ockham and Luis de Molina Would Have Said to Nuel Belnap: A Discussion of Some Arguments Against 'The Thin Red Line,'" *Nuel Belnap on Indeterminism and Free Action*, ed. Thomas Müller (New York: Springer, 2014).
Figure 6. Matthew Ritchie, 2016.
Figure 7. Ramon Llull, "Liber de Ascensu et Decensu Intellectus," 1303.
Figure 8. From Giovanni Arrighi, *The Long Twentieth Century: Money, Power and the Origins of Our Times* (Verso: 2010), 220.
Figure 9. From Isaac Newton, *Opticks; or, A Treatise of the Reflexions, Refractions, Inflexions and Colours of Light* . . . (London: Printed for Sam. Smith & Benj. Walford . . . , 1704), bk. 1, pt. 2, pl. 3, fig. 11.
Figure 10. From Isaac Newton, *Philosophiæ Naturalis Principia Mathematica*, Book 3, *De mundi systemate* (London: Royal Society, 1726), 135.
Figure 11. From Michel Foucault, *The Order of Things: An Archaeology of the Human Sciences* (New York: Pantheon Books, 1971), 201.
Figure 12. From Thomas Malton, *A Compleat Treatise on Perspective, in Theory and Practice* . . . , 2d. ed. (London: Printed for the author . . . , 1775), pl. IV.
Figure 13. Houston Stewart Chamberlain, *Immanuel Kant; A Study and a Comparison with Goethe, Leonardo da Vinci, Bruno, Plato and Descartes*, trans. Algernon Bertram Freeman-Mitford Redesdale (London: John Lane, 1914).
Figure 14. From William Blake, *Milton, A Poem*, 1810, Rosenwald Collection, Library of Congress Washington, D.C., Copy D, object 32, ca. 1818.
Figure 15. From John Venn, *Symbolic Logic* (London: MacMillan & Co, 1881).
Figure 16. From Edgar Allan Poe, *Eureka, A Prose Poem* (New York: Putnam, 1848), 50.
Figure 17. From Frederik Stjernfelt, *Diagrammatology: An Investigation on the Borderlines of Phenomenology, Ontology, and Semiotics* (Heidelberg: Springer, 2007), 306.
Figure 18. Charles Darwin's tree diagram. From Charles Darwin, Notebook B, 1837, Cambridge University Library, p. 36.
Figure 19. From James Mensch, "A Brief Account of Husserl's Doctrine of Time Consciousness," paper, 2013.
Figure 20. From *The Scientific Letters and Papers of James Clerk Maxwell*, vol. 3, 1874–79, ed. P. M. Harman (Cambridge: Cambridge University Press, 2002), 232 (pl. IV).
Figure 21. From A. Ya. Lerner, *Fundamentals of Cybernetics*, trans. E. Gros (New York: Plenum Pub. Corp., 1975), 257.
Figure 22. From Hermann Minkowski, "Raum und Zeit," *Jahresbericht der Deutschen Mathematiker-Vereinigung* 18 (1909): 82 (fig. 2).
Figure 23. From Jean Baptiste Perrin, *Les Atomes* (New York: D. Van Nostrand Co., 1916), 115 (fig. 6).
Figure 24. From Paul Klee, *Pedagogical Sketchbook* [1925], trans. Sibyl Moholy-Nagy (London: Faber & Faber, 1953), 35 (fig. 30).
Figure 25. From Marcel Duchamp, *Á l'infinitif* (New York: Cordier & Brown, 1966).
Figure 26. Max Ernst, *Let There Be Fashion, Down With Art!*, 1920, pl. VI.
Figure 27. From Reza Negarestani, *Cyclonopedia: Complicity with Anonymous Materials* (Melbourne: re.press, 2008), 28.
Figure 28. From Richard P. Feynman, "A Space-Time Approach to Quantum Electrodynamics," *Physical Review* 76, no. 6 (1949): 772 (fig. 1).
Figure 29. From Max Tegmark, "The Multiverse Hierarchy," in Bernard Carr, ed., *Universe or Multiverse?* (Cambridge: Cambridge University Press, 2007), 117.
Figure 30. From the notebook of Francis Crick, Sketch of the DNA double helix, 1953, pencil drawing. Wellcome Library, Francis Crick Archive.
Figure 31. From E. C. Zeeman, "Catastrophe Theory," *Scientific American* 234 (April 1976): 65–83.
Figure 32. From Edward N. Lorenz, "Deterministic Nonperiodic Flow," *Journal of the Atmospheric Sciences* 20, no. 2 (1963): 137.
Figure 33. Joseph Beuys, *Letter To London*, 1977.
Figure 34. Mel Bochner, Diagram for *48" around the Room*, 1969.
Figure 35. From Rosalind Krauss, "Sculpture and the Expanded Field," *October* 8 (Spring 1979): 37.
Figure 36. *The First Four Nodes of the Internet* (then called the ARPANET), by Lawrence Roberts, 1969.

Figure 37. From Bruno Latour, *We Have Never Been Modern*, trans. Catherine Porter (Cambridge, MA: Harvard University Press, 1993), Figure 3.3, 58.
Figure 38. The Internet, ca. 2015. Found at https://en.wikipedia.org/wiki/ICANN#/media/File:Internet_map_1024_-_transparent,_inverted.png
Figure 39. From Reka Albert and Albert-László Barabási, "Topology of Evolving Networks: Local Events and Universality," *Physical Review Letters* 85, no. 24 (2000): 5235.
Figure 40. From Ginestra Bianconi and Albert-László Barabási, "Bose-Einstein Condensation in Complex Networks," *Physical Review Letters* 86, no. 24 (2001): 5633.
Figure 41. Matthew Ritchie, 2016.
Figure 42. Matthew Ritchie, 2015.
Figure 43. From Graham Harman, *The Quadruple Object* (Arlesford: Zero Books, 2011), 79.
Figure 44. From Lorraine Daston and Peter Galison, *Objectivity* (New York: Zone Books, 2007), 371.
Figure 45. From Jürg Fröhlich, "Einstein and h: Advances in Quantum Mechanics," in *Einstein for the 21st Century: His Legacy in Science, Art, and Modern Culture*, ed. Peter Galison et al. (Princeton: Princeton University Press, 2008), 262.
Figure 46. Sketch by Nima Arkani-Hamed. From "A Jewel at the Heart of Quantum Physics," *Quanta Magazine*, September 17, 2013.
Figure 47. Will Steffen et al., "Planetary Boundaries: Guiding Human Development on a Changing Planet," *Science* 347, no. 6223 (February 13, 2015).
Figure 48. Matthew Ritchie, 2015.
Figure 49. From Tianjun Li et al., "The F-Landscape: Dynamically Determining the Multiverse," *Int. J. Mod. Phys.* A27 (2012): 1250121, MIFPA 11-49, fig. 1.
Figure 50. Matthew Ritchie, 2015.
Figure 51. "Mori Uncanny Valley" by Smurrayinchester, self-made, based on image by Masahiro Mori and Karl MacDorman at http://www.androidscience.com/theuncannyvalley/proceedings2005/uncannyvalley.html. Licensed under CC BY-SA 3.0 via Commons - https://commons.wikimedia.org/wiki/File:Mori_Uncanny_Valley.svg#/media/File:Mori_Uncanny_Valley.svg.
Figure 52. From www.openthefuture.com/2007/10/the_second_uncanny_valley.html.
Figure 53. From Denise L. Herzing, "Profiling Nonhuman Intelligence: An Exercise in Developing Unbiased Tools for Describing Other Types of Intelligence on Earth," *Acta Astronautica* 94, no. 2 (2014): 676–80.
Figure 54. Matthew Ritchie, 2016.
Figure 55. From Caroline A. Jones, "The Mediated Sensorium," in *Sensorium: Embodied Experience, Technology, and Contemporary Art*, ed. Caroline A. Jones (Cambridge, MA: MIT Press, 2006), 6.
Figure 56. Matthew Ritchie, 2016.
Figure 57. Matthew Ritchie, 2012.
Figures 58–64. Matthew Ritchie, 2016.

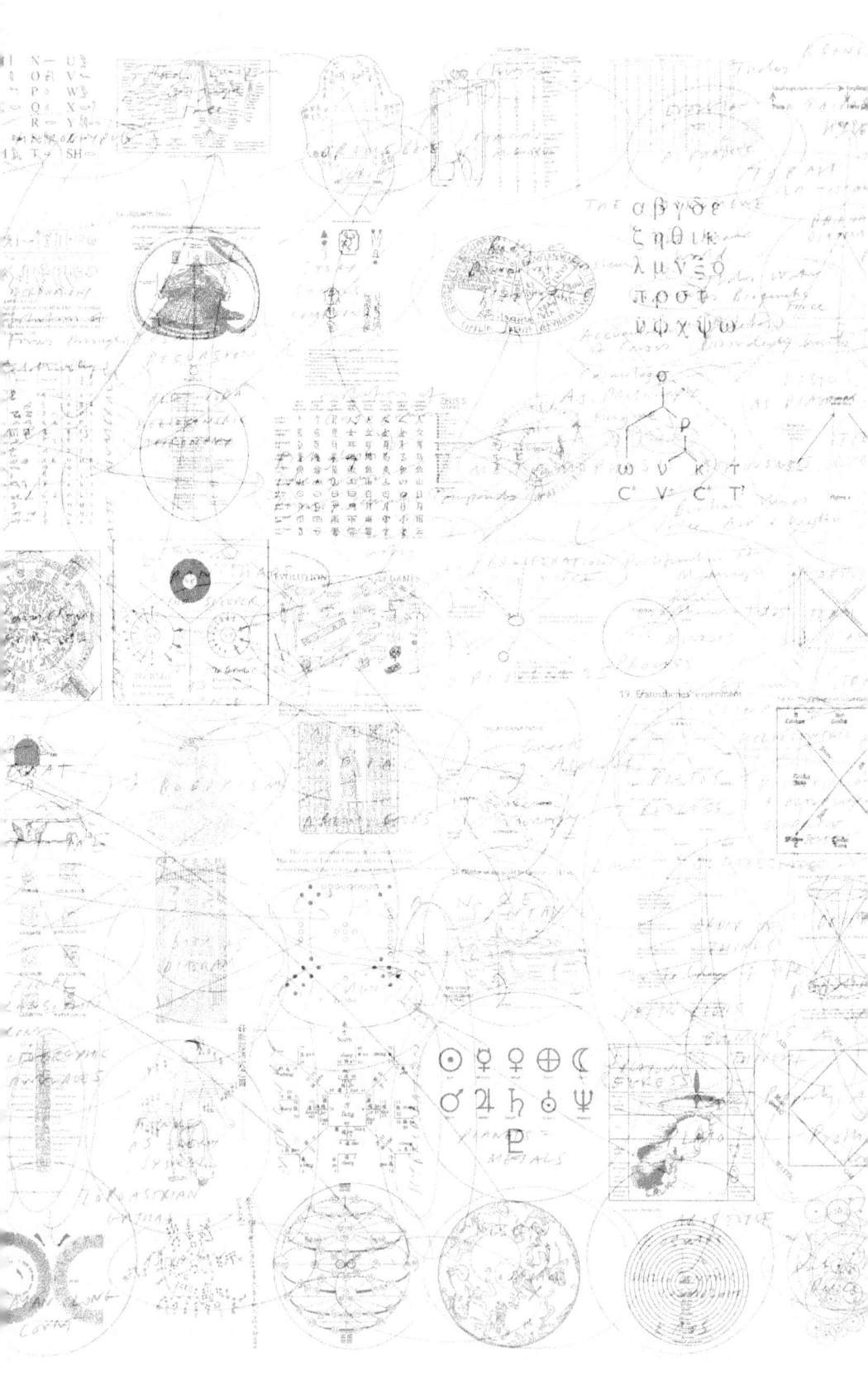

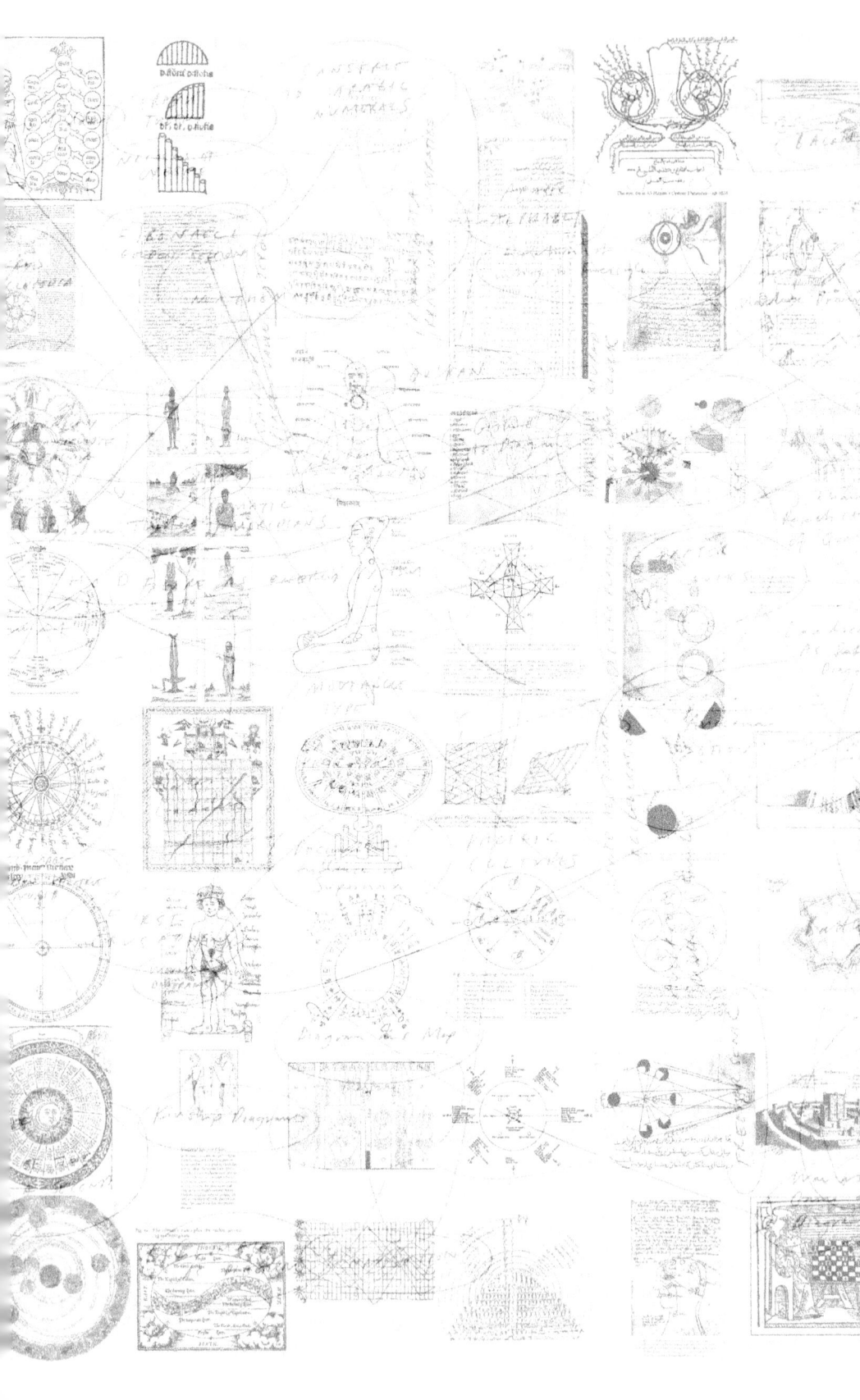

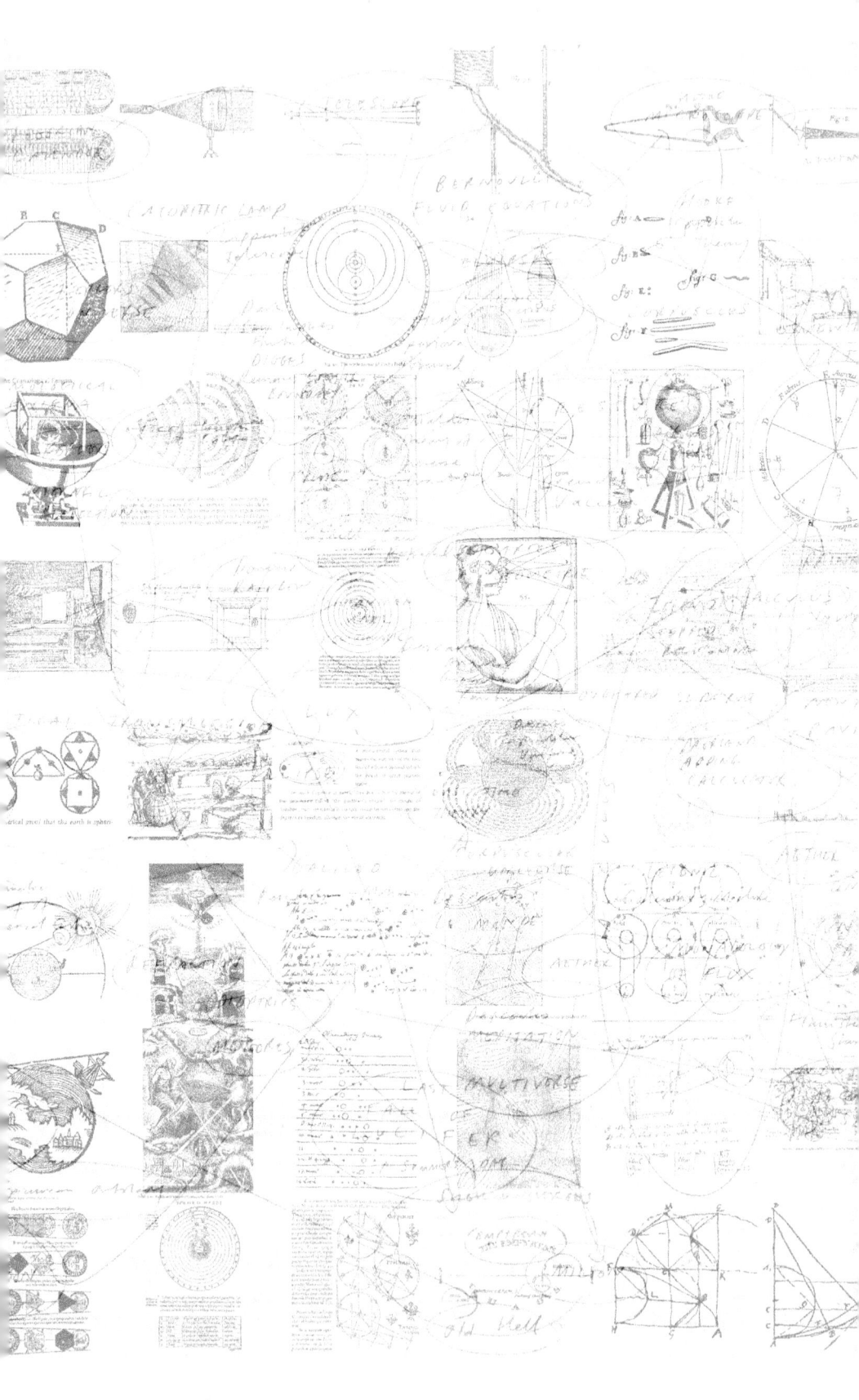

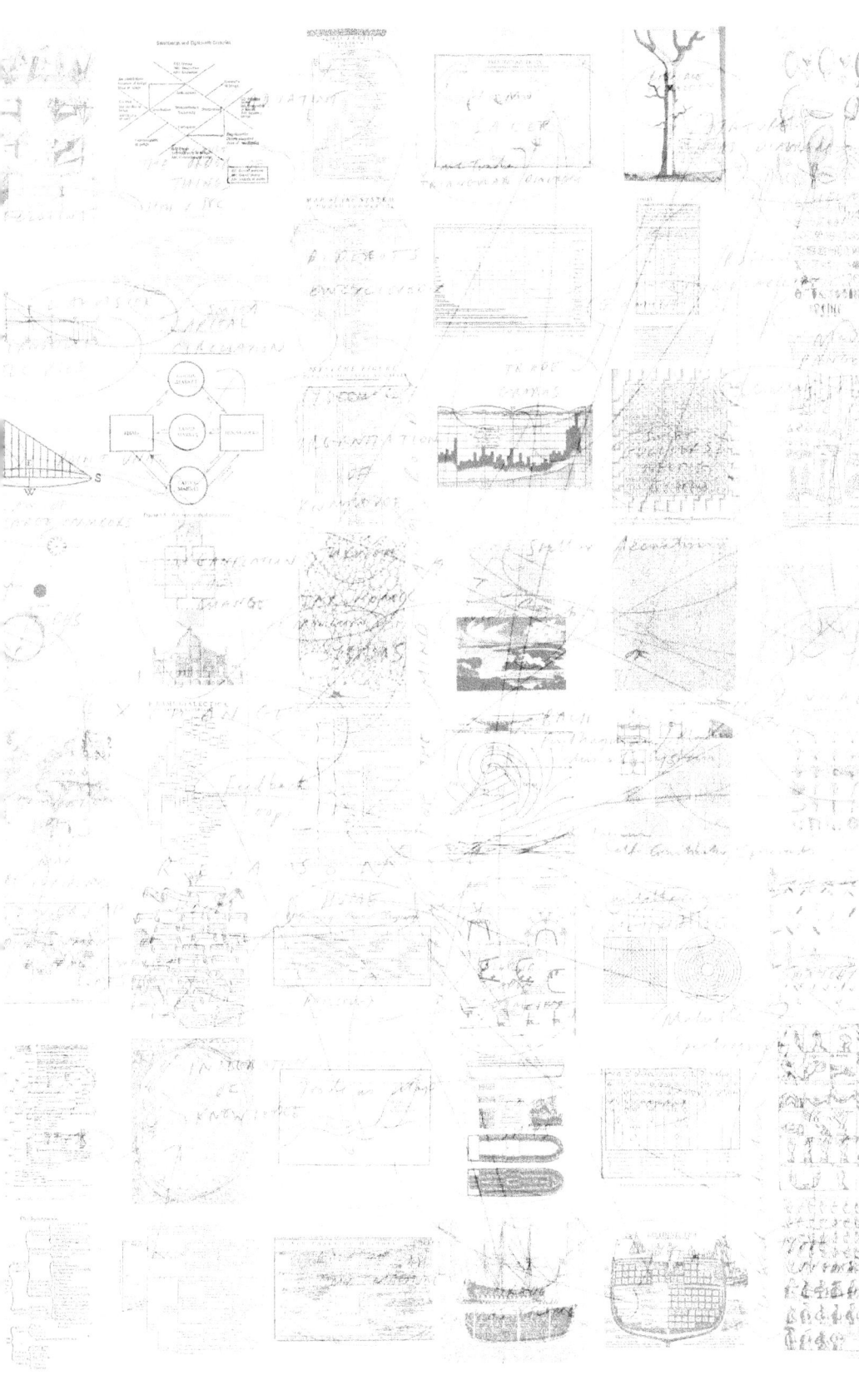

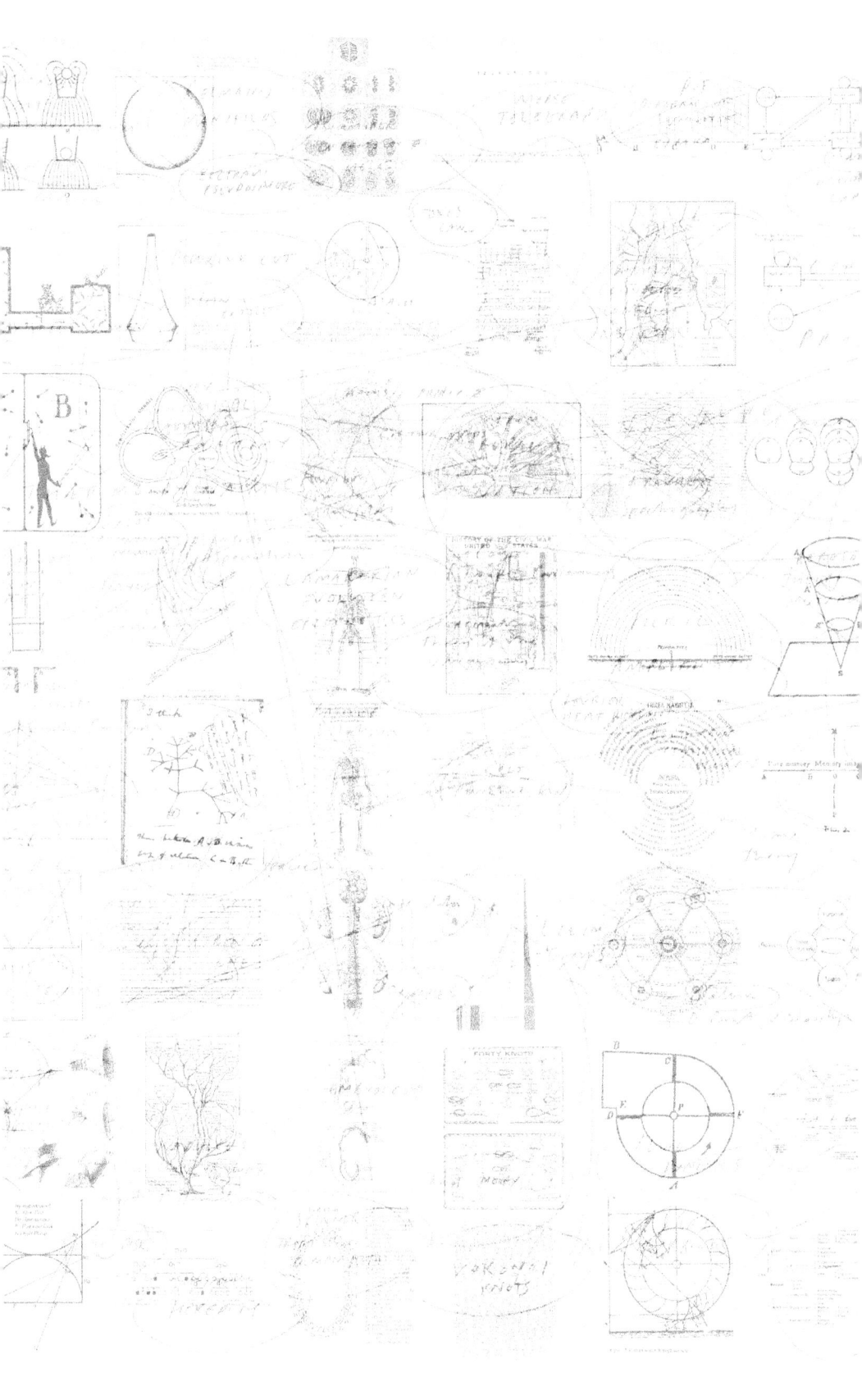

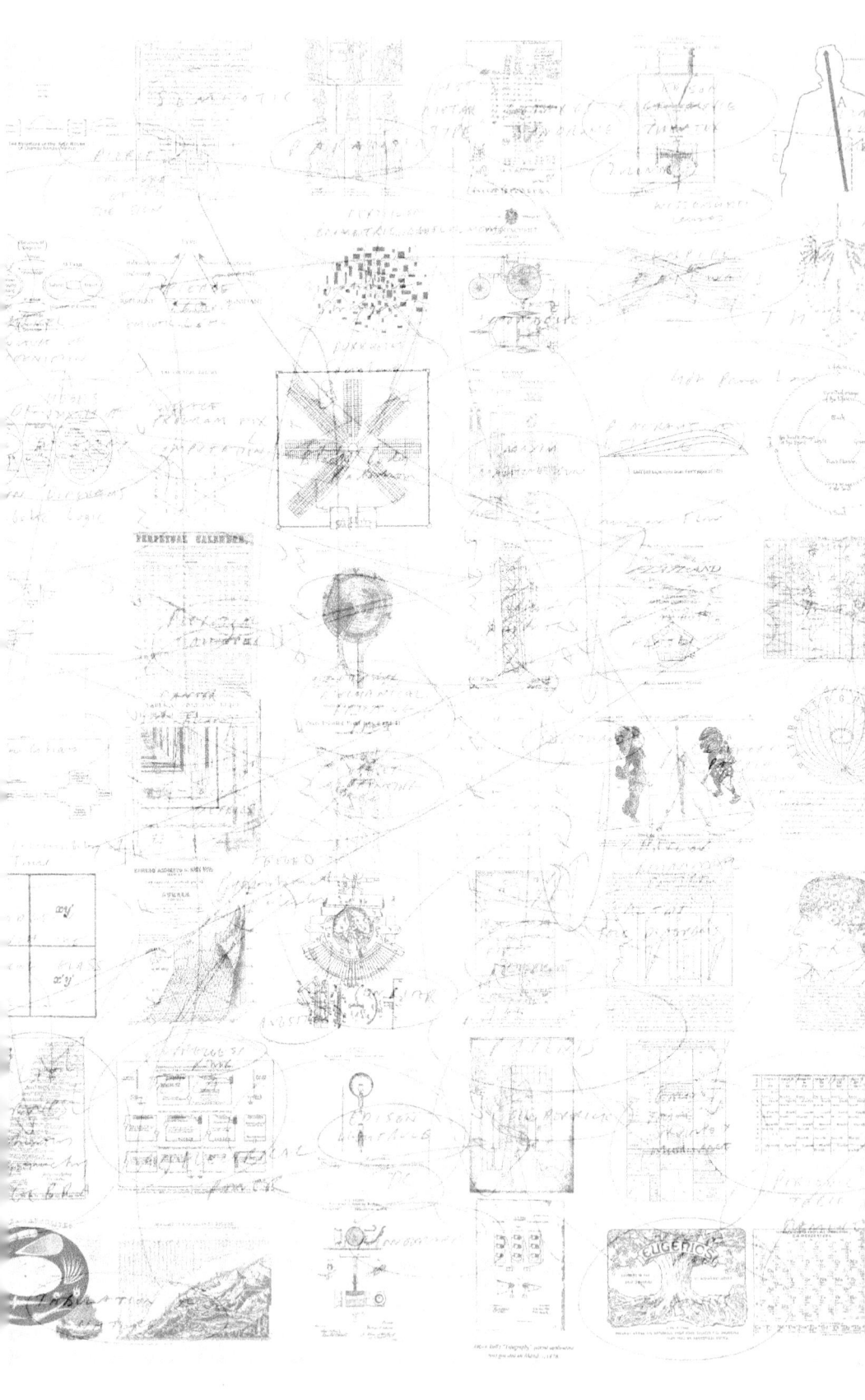

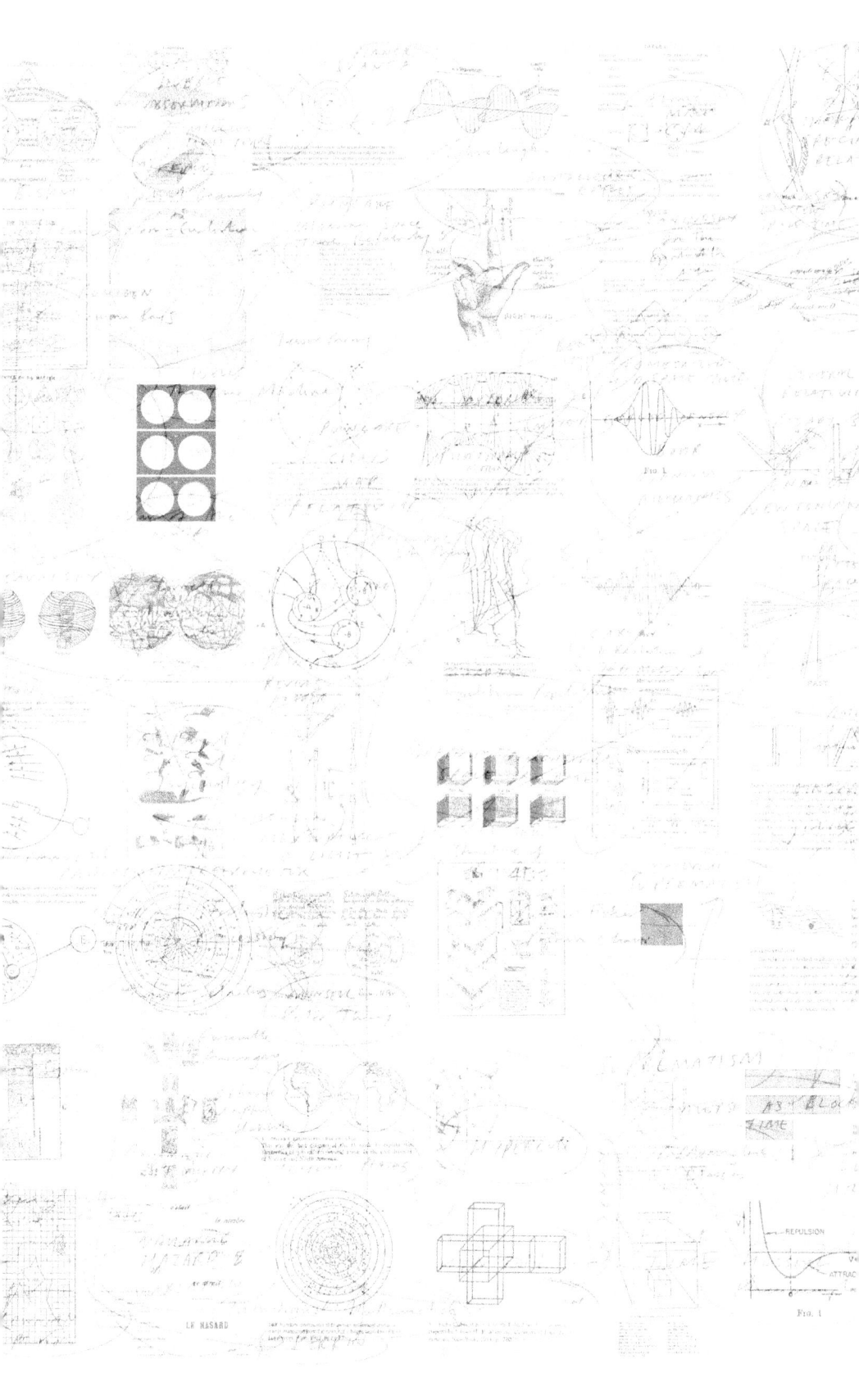

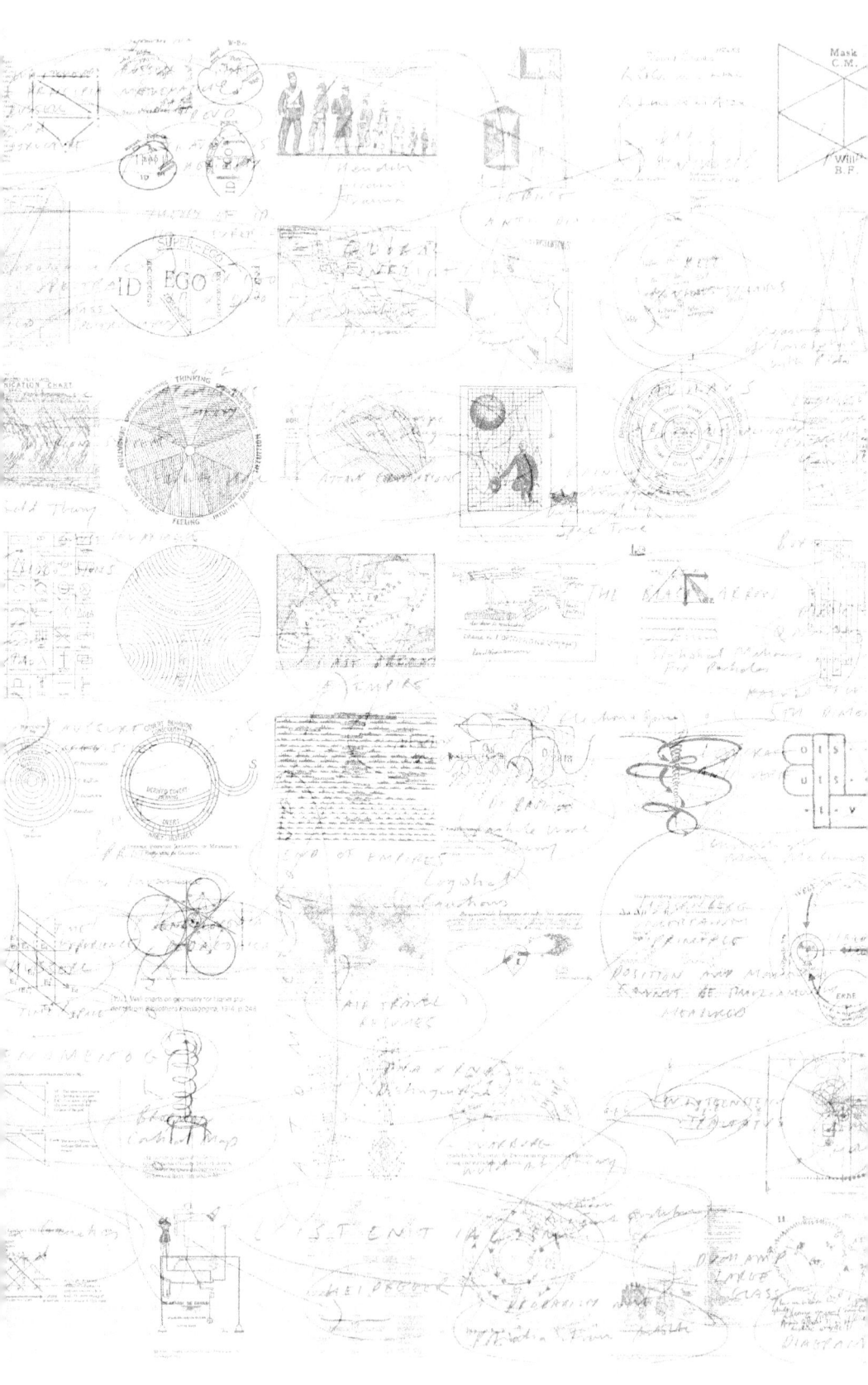

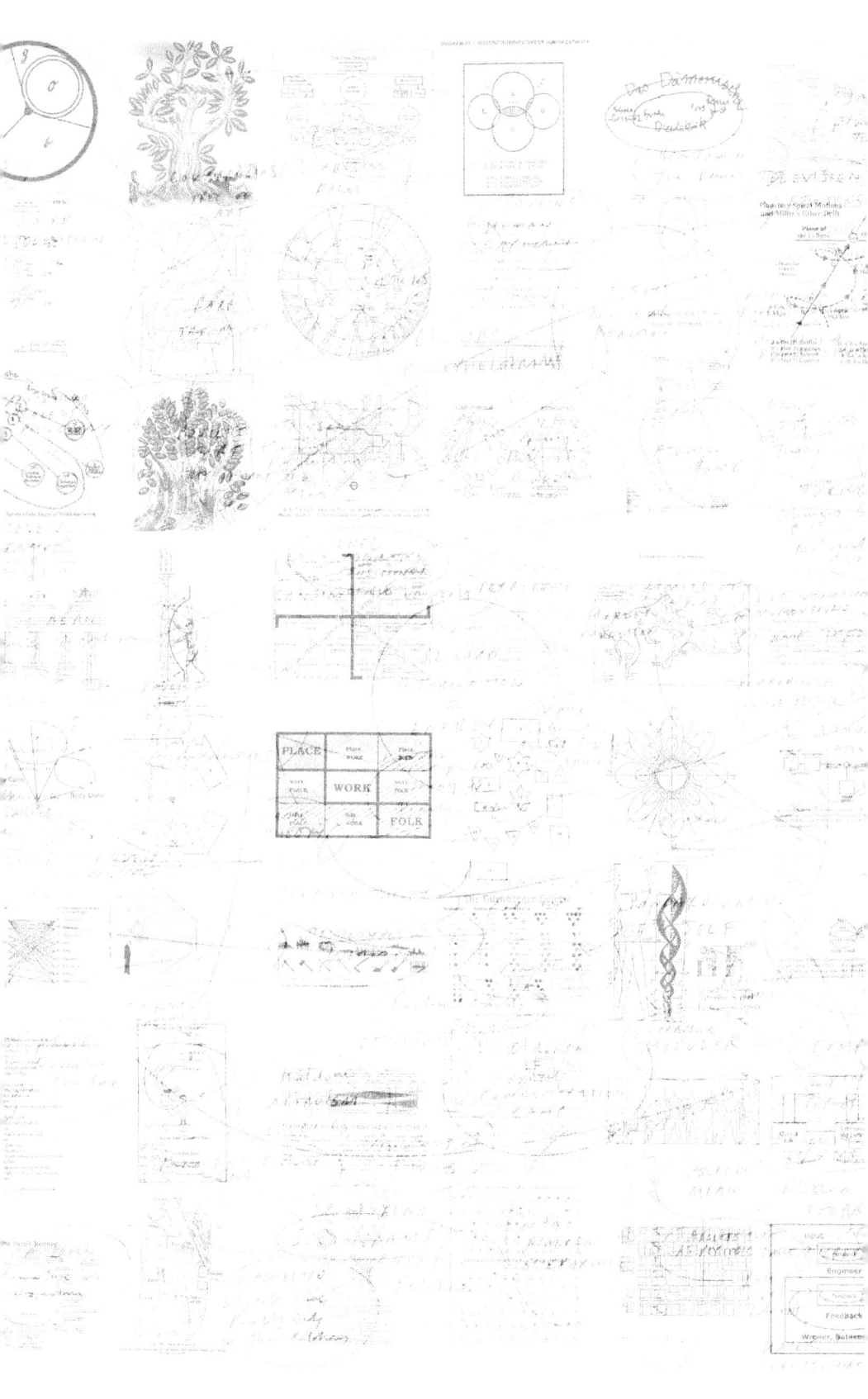

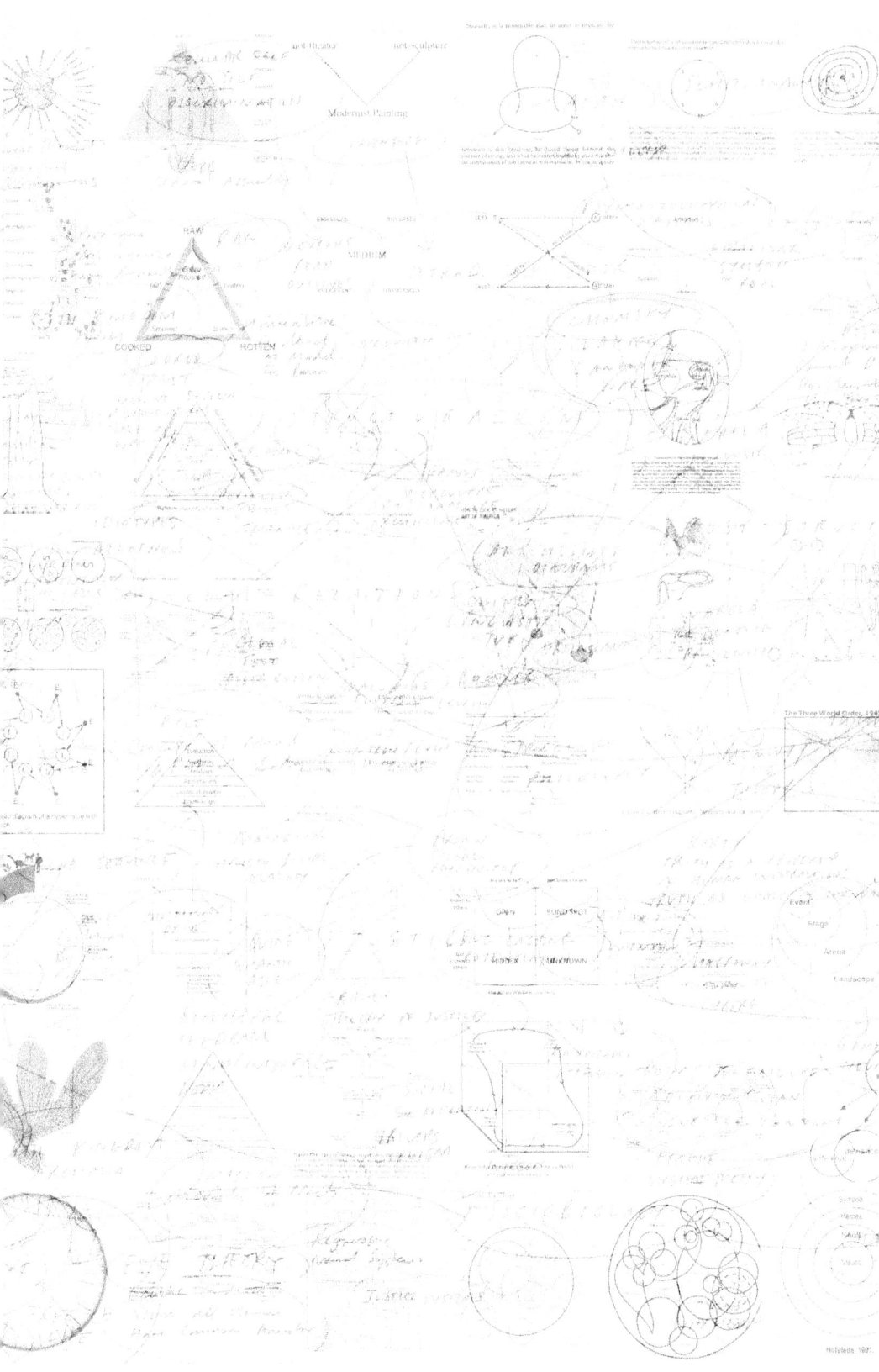

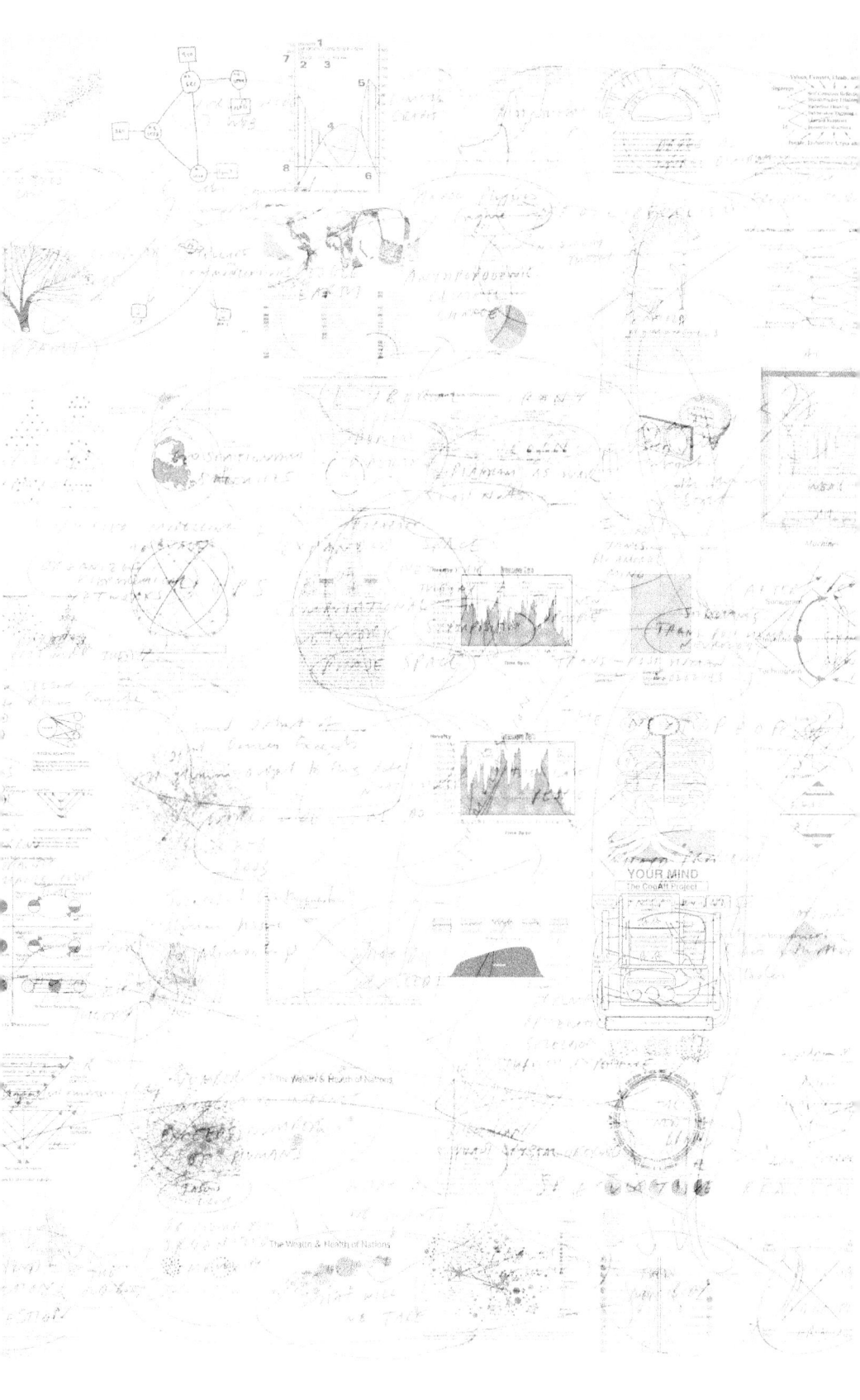

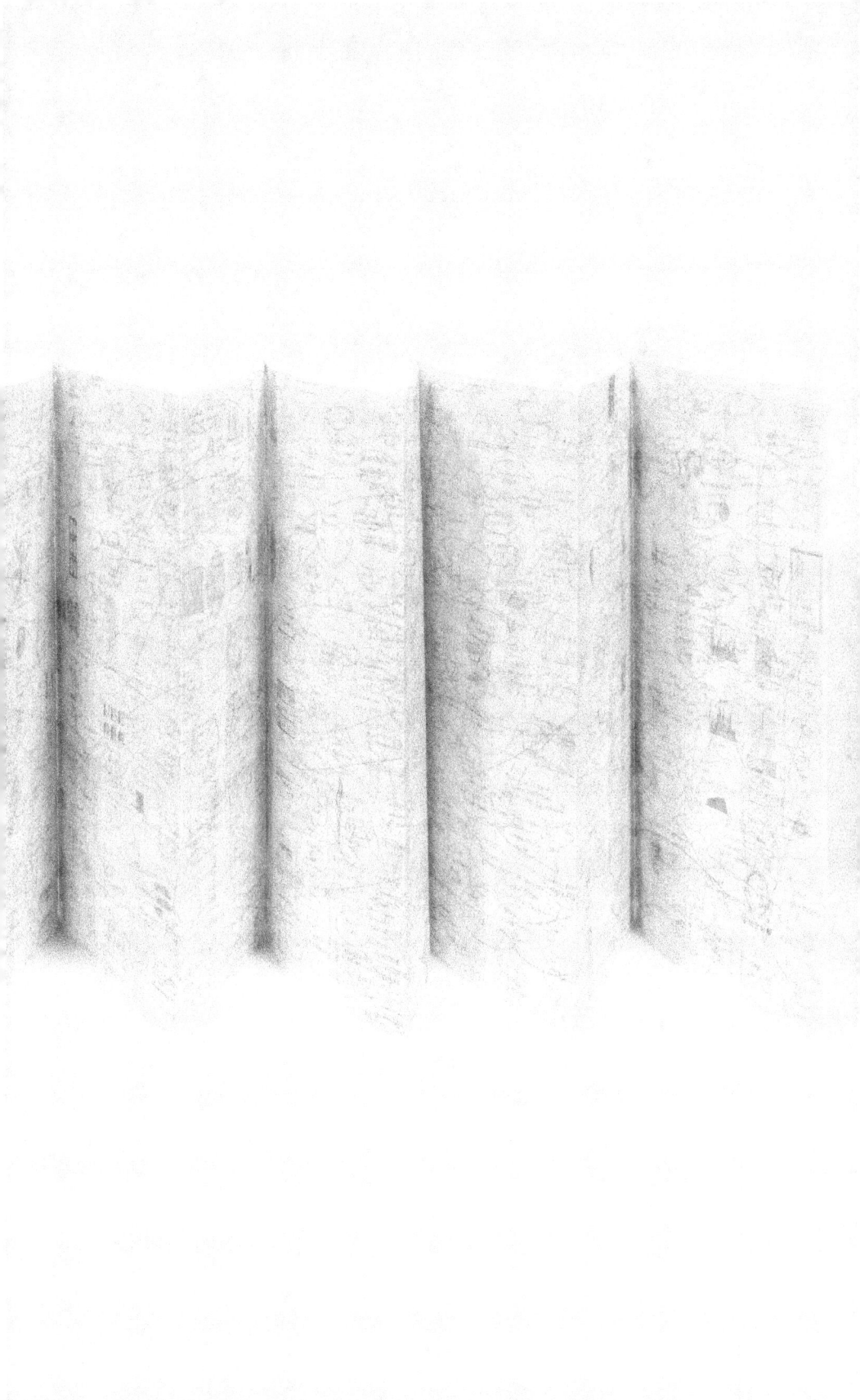

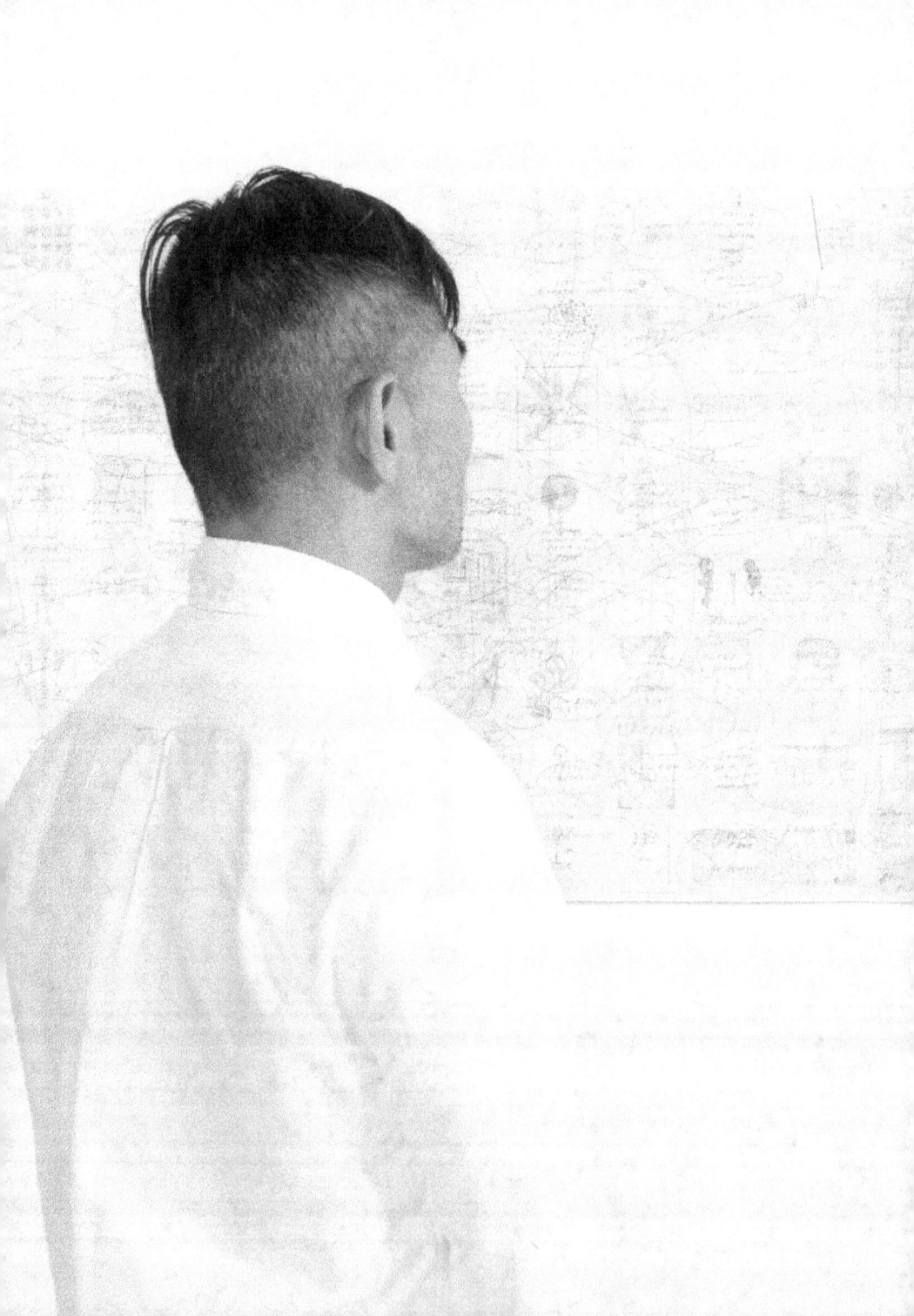

Schematic Aspects of an Aesthetics of Diagrams

Frederik Stjernfelt

What could diagrams possibly have to do with aesthetics or the arts? The prototypical diagram is a stylized graphical model facilitating interrelated information about some subject—hence, as a tendency, pragmatic, no-nonsense, fact-oriented, obvious. Facilitating the retrieval of information—scientific, political, practical, or otherwise—diagrams seem to emphasize direct accessibility over aesthetic depth and elaboration of representations.

This first consideration, however, conceals certain complications.

1.
Diagrammatic perception. A first thing to note is that ordinary perception has certain diagrammatic qualities. Contrary to a widespread commonsense (and sometimes phenomenological) conception, perception does not simply consist of 100 percent determinate, particular sense data—so that all sorts of general content or schematic structure should be something derivative, pertaining to secondary, higher-order cognitive processing. Rather, the structuring of perceptive contents is part and parcel of the perception process and, in the central example of vision, begins already in the retina. Thus, central features like contour enhancement begin with interaction between retinal cells, and the basic distinction of *where* and *what* in the visual field is provided by the basic structural separation of the dorsal (*where*) stream and the ventral (*what* or *how*) stream of visual processing in the brain. The former continuously updates structural information about immediate environmental space in terms of attention, object borders, accessibility, and so on. The latter continuously categorizes objects and events within that space. Each of these has diagrammatical qualities. The former structures space into connected subspaces and thus lays the foundation of the ability to articulate and rationally connect a spatial whole into parts, which is so central to the understanding of diagrams. The latter involves the schematic representations of the semantics of categories—the basic visual structure of chairs, tables, birds, clouds, and all the mesoscopic inventory of our surroundings, which we categorize automatically without

explicitly intending it. These processes—and many more—yield the highly structured character of the resulting visual perception experience. It contains many diagrammatic aspects, even if we may not realize it at every glance—accustomed as we are to its appearance. But those diagrammatic aspects of experience are what allows us to draw immediate inferences from it and act in a matter of moments—as well as to draw more complicated, longer-lasting inferences from certain perceptions, which merit our more detailed attention. But it is not as if we could "switch off" these ongoing structurings and fall back on the unstructured, fleeting experience of the simple flow of incoming light.

2.
Diagrammatic picture qualities. When making pictures, including diagrams, we may choose to further emphasize such features of perceptual content as have already been highlighted in the perceptual process. This gives pictures and images of all sorts a potential degree of further diagrammatization. Contour enhancement may be further strengthened, for example, by means of the addition of contour lines. Stylization may simplify and typify the representation of categorized objects so as to make them easier to recognize—or more general in their reference. Discretization may simplify the amount of colors and shapes used to conform to a smaller repertoire of such selected features. Selecting the right moment of an action, from which an optimum of information about the near past and future of the process may be inferred (Lessing's principle, as it were). Compactifying several different moments within one picture may represent a diagrammatical timeline, facilitating the reconstruction of a longer process beyond the immediate snapshot quality of representing a moment. Thus, the amount of diagrammatic qualities in ordinary perception is typically (not always) only increased in pictorial representation. Of course, artistic strategies may take as their aim, rather, to *minimize* diagrammatic representation by all sorts of blurring, ambiguization, abstraction (in the painterly rather than the logical sense of the word).

3.
Diagrams proper. Thus we arrive at diagrammatic representations proper—typically: explicitly articulated graphical structures on screen, blackboard, paper—realizing that in a certain sense, they form the tip of the iceberg only. Diagrammaticality is already there in perception; it typically increases in pictures and images only to reach full, explicit, and often intended expression in charts, maps, matrices, tables, block or pie charts, curves, graphs, and so on. Diagrams in this sense have been known since antiquity and reached an early apogee in Euclid.

Diagrams in this sense express wholes composed from rationally related parts, where the rational relations are represented by spatial position, sequence, connection, continuity, and so on. Diagrams presuppose abstractions in the sense that they represent a few selected properties only of the object they depict—those properties are subsequently idealized and made the focus of the diagram. Topographical maps constitute an exemplary case: they depict selected landscape features such as buildings, roads, forests, lakes, elevation, and coastlines while other landscape features and variations are abstracted away. This generalization inherent in diagrams implies that, very often, a diagram holds for a number of individual cases: the topographical map, unlike the aerial photograph, does not refer to landscape conditions in one single moment only, but holds for a whole period, that is, an indefinite number of moments, until landscape changes make it invalid. The object of the diagram is thus more or less general—but generality also characterizes the diagram sign itself. It may be reproduced in a number of variations without ceasing to be the same diagram. This may be expressed, also in the opposite direction, so to speak: the individual diagram token as printed on a page or emitting light from your computer screen, occurring in the present now, constitutes a window to the more general diagram type that it represents. Diagrams thus make possible the direct contemplation of general subject matters. This quality is a basic reason for their pragmatic ubiquity: they facilitate the easy grasp of a complicated matter of fact in one or a few gazes. But their generality has several sources: one is the graphical formalism in itself—idealized, stylized, simplified as it is. Another is the accompanying (or implicit) symbolic information, which indicates the type of diagram and type of object referred to. Take Harry Beck's famous 1931 London Underground Map, with its continuously updated versions in use to this day, arguably one of the world's most famous diagrams. For a first user, the text "London Underground" gives the double information that this spaghetti of colored lines should be read as referring to the structure of subterranean city train lines. This indicates how the diagram should be read, in general. Thus, diagrams generalize Kant's famous definition of a *schema*: it unites spatiotemporal representation with symbolic understanding of the entity represented. The spatiotemporal layout of the diagram plus the indication of what type of object it represents unite to perform that function.

An as-yet-unsolved question with regard to diagrams pertains to their subtypes: is there a rational taxonomy of diagram types? Charles S. Peirce proposed, as a first hypothesis, that they comprise maps, algebras, and graphs. The appearance of algebras in this list may surprise, as they are not typically regarded as diagrams in our ordinary parlance.

The reason for this lies in his important observation that diagrams may facilitate reasoning.

4.
Diagrams as vehicles for reasoning. To Peirce, diagrams comprise all structures that are fit for one to make deductive inferences from. In the topographical map, for example, you may trace possible routes from one location to another—thus inferring information that was only implicitly present in the diagram. The routes thus found are truly there as real possibilities in the landscape, given that the map as a premise is, in itself, a true representation of the landscape (if the map is false, of course, you can not be sure to draw true conclusions from it). Thus, Peirce's argument is that diagrams form the proper generalization of the various formalisms of deductive logic. And this is why algebras, to him, come under the headline of diagrams: algebraically expressed states-of-affairs may be used to infer other truths—for example, an arithmetic equation, algebraically expressed, may be solved. Diagrams are ideal models with deductive possibilities.

This implies that diagrams, as signs, differ in important ways from the pneumatic-dispatch model of communication: the idea that the sender has an intended claim, codes it in a message which is, in turn, decoded by the receiver. In diagrams, the manipulation or experimentation with the diagram icon makes possible the retrieval of information from the diagram that was never explicitly put there by the sender. There is no reason to believe that the producer of maps has already calculated, for example, the distance between any two points of interest on the map—or any other particular information which may be deduced from the map. Diagrams, of course, differ enormously as to the extent implicit knowledge is derivable from them. Some diagrams, such as topographical maps, seem to have an indefinite amount of information that may be inferred from them. Others, such as algebraic equations, may in some cases remain unsolved; it has not yet been established whether important knowledge may be derived from them. In any case, the fact that diagrams hold implicit information, simple or complex, easy or difficult to derive, is probably what gives them their immediate appearance of *depth*—something is, to some degree, concealed here, and it may require work to derive it and make it appear.

5.
Diagram subtypes. Are all diagrams graphic? Indeed, graphically expressed, two-dimensional visual diagrams form the core of our everyday diagram conception, but for a closer gaze, it is not obvious

that the rational category of diagrams is thus delimited. If diagrams are all formalisms from which implicit information may be derived, there is no reason why diagrams may not exist in other sense modalities. In particular, spoken language may represent a large number of one-dimensional diagrams in an auditory, temporal medium, which overlaps with the one-dimensional visual, spatial medium of linear writing. Tactile diagrams are used by blind people. So one range of subtypes of diagrams is that of their different sensory representations. Here should also be counted *imagined* diagrams—whole diagrams up to some threshold of complexity (which is probably highly individually variable) may be imagined and manipulated before the mind's eye. And, in many cases, the use of externalized diagrams on paper or screen requires use of the imagination. Quick inferences may be drawn from maps by means of imagined manipulations of them rather than real, physical manipulation.

A basic distinction is that between pure and applied diagrams. The London Underground Map can be seen as a purely topological network structure if we bracket both the general interpretation of it as depicting train lines and its indexical reference to the particular city of London. In that case, it is a purely topological object whose general properties may be investigated. What is found on that pure, general level will be inherited by the virtual applied uses of the structure, for instance, to refer to those subway trains running under London. Thus, all applied diagrams have a formal spatial structure whose possible transformations may be studied in and of themselves, regardless of application.

Another important distinction is probably that between continuous and discontinuous diagrams. Topographical maps are continuous in the sense that any full-dimension part of them is also, in itself, a map—which is not the case with algebraic expressions or other diagrams using symbol sequences on a line or in a matrix.

A further distinction is dimensionality. Human language, spoken or written, interpreted as diagrams, is in a certain sense one-dimensional, just like many logic or algebraic languages. The most typical diagrams are probably two-dimensional—maps, charts, Cartesian planes, and so on—but there seems to be no a priori reason why diagrams could not have any dimensionality. In particular, idealized three-dimensional models inherit the easy accessibility with whole-part structure, the derivability of information by (imagined) manipulation and so on.

6.
Aesthetics of diagrams. What has been said until now is probably the very least needed to be reflected on before, by means of hypotheses, some aesthetic possibilities pertaining to diagrams may be discussed.

First—depending, of course, on use, materials, context, reference, style, and other expressive variants—a number of potential aesthetic qualities of diagrams, exploitable for artistic purposes, may be listed. Unavoidably, some of the qualities here indicated will overlap.

Abstractness. Diagrams are abstract in at least two ways. First, they abstract away certain variant or irrelevant aspects or properties of the object they depict. Second, the properties and relations selected are, themselves, subjected to an idealization, which may sometimes also be called abstraction. "Abstraction" in twentieth-century high modernism often approaches diagrammatic qualities.

Analyticity. Diagrams not only select certain properties, they also analyze them and their mutual relations. Diagrams do not display object parts, properties, and relations isolated from each other. Rather, they portray them in (some of) their interrelations; that is, the diagram as a whole synthesizes, in turn, the parts first analyzed.

Arrows. Far from all diagrams use arrows; however, many do. Arrows may mean rather different things. They may signify some relation between two parts connected by them, be it a temporal, spatial, or semantic relation. They may, for example, signify a cause-effect relationship, an oriented flow of material or energy, an intention, a dependence, or an inference.

Constructivity. Diagrams are constructs of the intellect. That does not make them constructivist; rather, the opposite. Diagrams are typically realist with respect to the aspects of some reality that they isolate. But their construction, simultaneously, hints at the intellect able to isolate those aspects and connect them in the proper manner. Depending upon the degree of simplicity or complexity of the diagram in question, this implicit intellect may be a simple mind or a genius; most often diagrams intimate a mind with analytic interests and powers.

Dots. Again, far from all diagrams use dots, but in those that do, dots typically indicate some entity that is a localized part of a larger structure, be it a person, a place, an institution . . . In maps, dots may be cities, mountaintops, depth of valleys, stations, the location of buried treasure, in short any place of particular interest. They may be categorized by means of a legend giving dots with particular shapes or colors particular meanings, or they may be described directly.

Economy. Diagrams are basically economical structures in the sense that they omit an immense amount of information in order to focus on the essential, thus serving economy of thought. In many cases, it is easier to make use of a diagram than of a full, detailed description of the same object, because in the diagram, irrelevant structures have already been filtered away, and the important and relevant information immediately leaps to the eye.

Essentialism. This word has had, for unknown reasons, a bad press recently, but there is really nothing wrong with searching for the essence of an object, which is just equivalent to those properties without which that object would cease to be that kind of object. The economy and abstraction of the diagram serves this purpose. Of course, like all signs, diagrams may be fallacious or even mendacious, in which case the purported essence is not real.

Filling in. The idea is that of the philosopher Roman Ingarden that in many cases, when confronted with ideal, indeterminate signs such as diagrams, the observer is called to fill in the *Leerstellen* (blanks) with more or less concrete, imagined realizations. This filling-in is undertaken from the observer's own fantasy, sometimes supported by indications found in or accompanying the diagram.

Fragility. The structural, skeletonized character of the diagram may, in many cases, give it a fragile expression—a frail composition of lines that may seem to be about to fall or disintegrate, if we (erroneously) interpret it as a real object.

Idealization. Diagrams not only abstract away properties deemed irrelevant, they also (unlike sketches) subject the remaining properties to idealization. This gives the diagram a sort of Platonic, outerworldly quality—as the deep reality behind many related appearances.

Imagination. Diagram use requires imagination. The individual diagram sign is not in itself ideal, consisting of physical lines and figures. So, in order to arrive at ideality, imagination must strip away irrelevant features of the diagram sign—for instance, often the color of lines is insignificant and the user must imagine a line with no particular color.

Indeterminacy. The very same quality as idealization, viewed from another angle, gives the diagram a certain openness. The fact that many properties of the object referred to are left indeterminate makes the diagram fit many possible concrete, particular cases and thus, in itself, gives it a quality of partial emptiness. Such emptiness may be taken in different directions, such as desolation on the one hand, or space of possibilities on the other.

Intersubjectivity. The diagram as an outer representation can be addressed, developed, and used by multiple persons at one and the same time, as well as sequentially over hours, days, centuries. This takes it far away from the idea of representations being only in the head, and gives it an optimistic air of collaboration, dialogue, and even possible progress. Simultaneously, when seeing a diagram, unlike natural objects, you know somebody has seen it before you did, and unlike most other cultural objects, you know it is indeterminate, unfinished, and that somebody, maybe you, could improve it.

Line. Probably the most widespread semantic tool of diagrams is that of lines. The signification of lines is really an issue of polysemy. Lines may signify all sorts of connection between their end points, they may signify contours of objects, they may signify opposition between the areas on each side of them, they may delimit an area of interest from one of irrelevance, and much more.

Manipulability. To Peirce, real or imagined manipulation is the key to retrieving implicit information from diagrams. The experimental manipulation with the diagram following certain rules, explicit or not, gives the user the possibility of inferring new claims from it which will be true, given that the information put into the diagram is true. This gives the diagram the character of an ideal machine. Its possession of implicit information also may give it a quasi-mystical quality of the looming presence of something not explicitly there.

Mereology. The diagram is a whole of connected parts, claiming to mirror the structure of a real or possible object. So, any diagram involves a double-, or multilayered, gaze: one, distant, giving the outline of the whole, the other, closer, giving the internal organization connecting parts of that whole, sometimes on several different, nested levels.

Objectivity. In most cases, diagrams are used to claim something about the structure of some object, event, or plan. That gives the diagram a cool, detached, objective, no-nonsense quality.

Overview. The mereological structure of the diagram implies that it may give the observer the overview of something otherwise difficult to synthesize. The object may be seen from impossible viewpoints, it may be dissected, analyzed, or laid out in counterintuitive ways in order to give that overview. Oftentimes, the overview may synthesize different temporal phases into one ideal glimpse of a whole sequential structure otherwise bound to stepwise experience.

Planning. Diagrams are often used as planning or construction tools due to their overview capabilities. That gives them, in many cases, a prospective quality of possibilities not yet realized, manipulation, or realization possibilities to come. Its use in planning, of course, may also carry less positive associations of compulsion, constraint, even exploitation or totalitarian politics.

Rationality. The analytical and inferential quality of diagrams, of course, give them an acute air of rationality. To Peirce, diagrams are simply tools with which to make deductions—the core of logic.

Regularity. The ideal quality of diagrams makes them, in a sense, rules for many individual realizations. Simultaneously, the manipulation of them relies on rules explicitly or implicitly given. This gives them a strong quality of regularity, which, importantly, does not conflict with their openness. This is due to the fact that their regularity is not that of an algorithm to be followed blindly; rather, it is like the rules of a game, facilitating an indefinite amount of games played.

Remoteness. The overview quality of diagrams also gives them, conversely, a certain remote quality. They conceive of their object from afar, making the observer (falsely?) at safe distance.

Schematicity. This is almost another word for diagrammaticity—however, with a stronger emphasis on their selective, skeleton-like character.

Scientificity. Diagrams have, of course, been used by most sciences, and often a scientific paper is built around one or a few central diagrams able to synthesize all of the conceptual preconditions and empirical findings into one irreducible whole the understanding of which often amounts to the understanding of the paper as a whole. Diagrams thus very often come with a strong association of science, discovery, experiment—but also the possible dullness and repetitive quality of secondary science.

Sheet. The white piece of paper or blank screen on which the diagram appears requires special attention. Peirce, in his "Existential Graphs" formalizing elementary logic, makes the sheet a universe of discourse, so to speak, an undeveloped photograph of all the implicit knowledge that the users of the diagram tacitly agree upon. Sometimes the sheet directly depicts the object—thus the surface of the earth in topographical diagrams. Sometimes it displays an ordered field of possibilities, like in an ordinary Cartesian plane. The empty page, in short, may mean rather different things; in any case, its blank quality gives the diagram a certain emptiness or, conversely, richness of possibilities.

Sketchiness. Sketches often have spontaneous diagrammatical qualities, so to speak on the way to full diagrams. Conversely, diagrams are typically sketched before they reach ideal completion. In any case, the individual diagram token sign invariably keeps certain irrelevant qualities, giving it a sketchy quality.

Slenderness. Oftentimes, the skeleton-like quality of the diagram gives it elegance, simplicity, delicacy—or emaciation.

Technicity. The affinity to planning and science points the diagram in the direction of technology. The diagram is, in itself, a technology of knowledge, of remembering, analyzing, synthesizing, inferring, but it may also be associated with other technologies for which it may serve as blueprint or construction device.

Unfinishedness. Openness and sketchiness may take the diagram in the direction of unfinishedness. More properties and relations of the object than actually selected could have been there—maybe, in some cases, they are lacking. Complicated diagrams may be works in progress over very long periods, like, for many centuries, the geographical task of the mapping of the earth.

Virtuality. The indefinite amount of implicit information in the diagram gives it a virtual, hypothetical quality, just like its ideality makes it an object different from ordinary, non-ideal, and determinate objects.

7.
Perspective. In a certain sense, all of these qualities are not isolated but are different aspects of the same diagram essence. Different designers, scientists, and artists may select or emphasize some of those aspects over others.

These qualities, then, may go into many different aesthetic strategies. Diagrams may be used as objets trouvés, exploiting their well-known or strange qualities as they appear. Diagrams may be cut up, suspending parts of full-blown diagrams to investigate effects of dysfunctional diagrams. Diagrams may be challenged by reconnecting diagrammatic structure with that substance from which they were abstracted in the first place, or by combining incompatible diagrams on the sheet. More generally, diagrams may be subject to all of the enormous toolbox of artistic strategies developed over 150 years of modernism. Those strategies, however, will exploit some of the possibilities sketched in this overview.

REFERENCE LIST

Ingarden, Roman. 1973. *The Literary Work of Art: An Investigation on the Borderlines of Ontology, Logic, and Theory of Literature*. Translated by George G. Grabowicz. Evanston: Northwestern University Press.
———. 1973a. *The Cognition of the Literary Work of Art*. Translated by Ruth Ann Crowley and Kenneth R. Olson. Evanston: Northwestern University Press.
Østergaard, Svend, and Stjernfelt, Frederik. 2013. "FONK! HONK! WHAM! OOF!: Representation of Events in Carl Barks—and in the Aesthetics of Comics in General." In *Picturing the Language of Images*, edited by Nancy Pedri, 483–508. Laurence Petit: Cambridge Scholars Press.
Peirce, Charles S. 1992. *The Essential Peirce: Selected Philosophical Writings*, vol. 1 (1867–1893). Edited by Nathan Houser and Christian Kloesel. Bloomington: Indiana University Press.
———. 1998. *Collected Papers of Charles Sanders Peirce*. 8 vols. Vols. 1–6 edited by Charles Hartshorne and Paul Weiss; vols. 7, 8 edited by Arthur Burks. Bristol: Thoemmes.
———. 1998a. *The Essential Peirce: Selected Philosophical Writings*, vol. 2 (1893–1913). Edited by Nathan Houser and Christian Kloesel. Bloomington: Indiana University Press.
Pietarinen, Ahti-Veikko. 2006. *Signs of Logic: Peircean Themes on the Philosophy of Language, Games, and Communication*. Dordrecht: Springer.
Shin, Sun-Joo. 2002. *The Iconic Logic of Peirce's Graphs*. Cambridge, MA: MIT Press.
Stjernfelt, Frederik. 2007. *Diagrammatology. An Investigation on the Borderlines of Phenomenology, Ontology, and Semiotics*. Dordrecht: Springer.
———. 2014. *Natural Propositions: The Actuality of Peirce's Doctrine of Dicisigns*. Boston: Docent.
———. 2015. "Green War Banners in Central Copenhagen: A Recent Political Struggle over Interpretation—and Some Implications for Art Interpretation as Such." In *Investigations into the Phenomenology and the Ontology of the Work of Art: What Are Artworks and How Do We Experience Them?*, edited by Peer Bundgaard and Frederik Stjernfelt, 209–24. Cham: Springer Open.

Following spreads: Matthew Ritchie. The Temptation of the Diagram, Installed at the Getty Research Institute, Los Angeles, 2018. Photos: John Kiffe © J Paul Getty Trust.

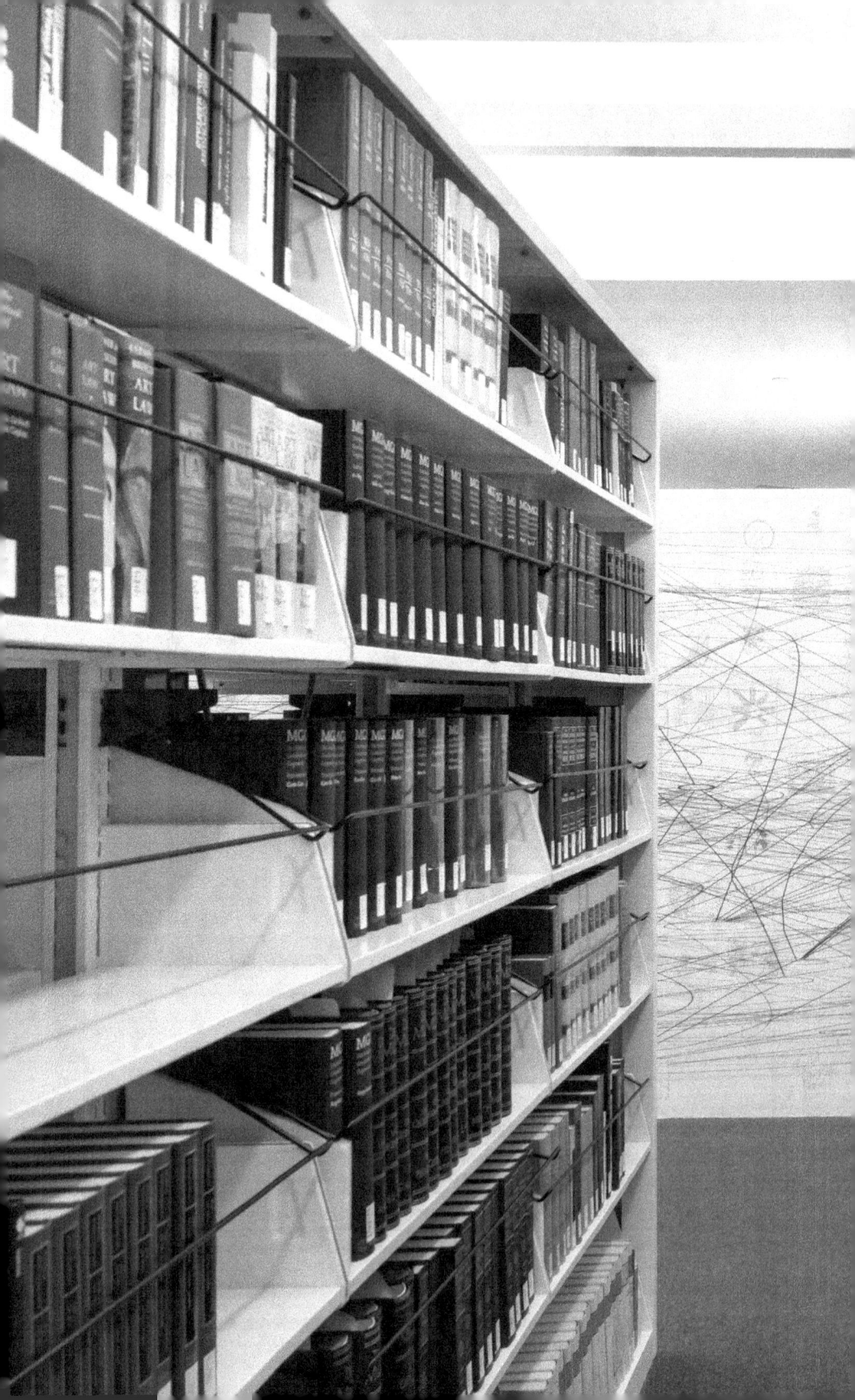

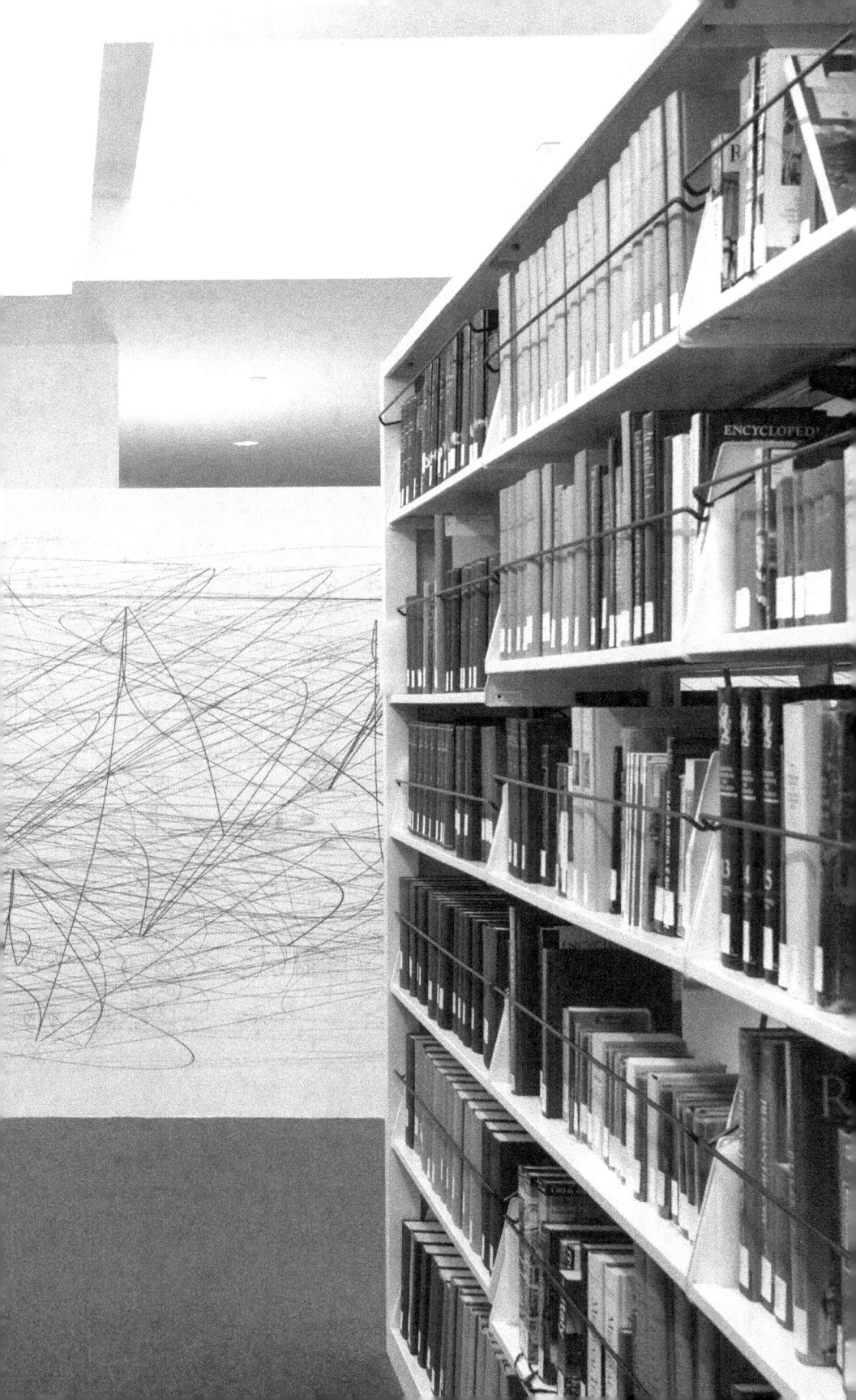

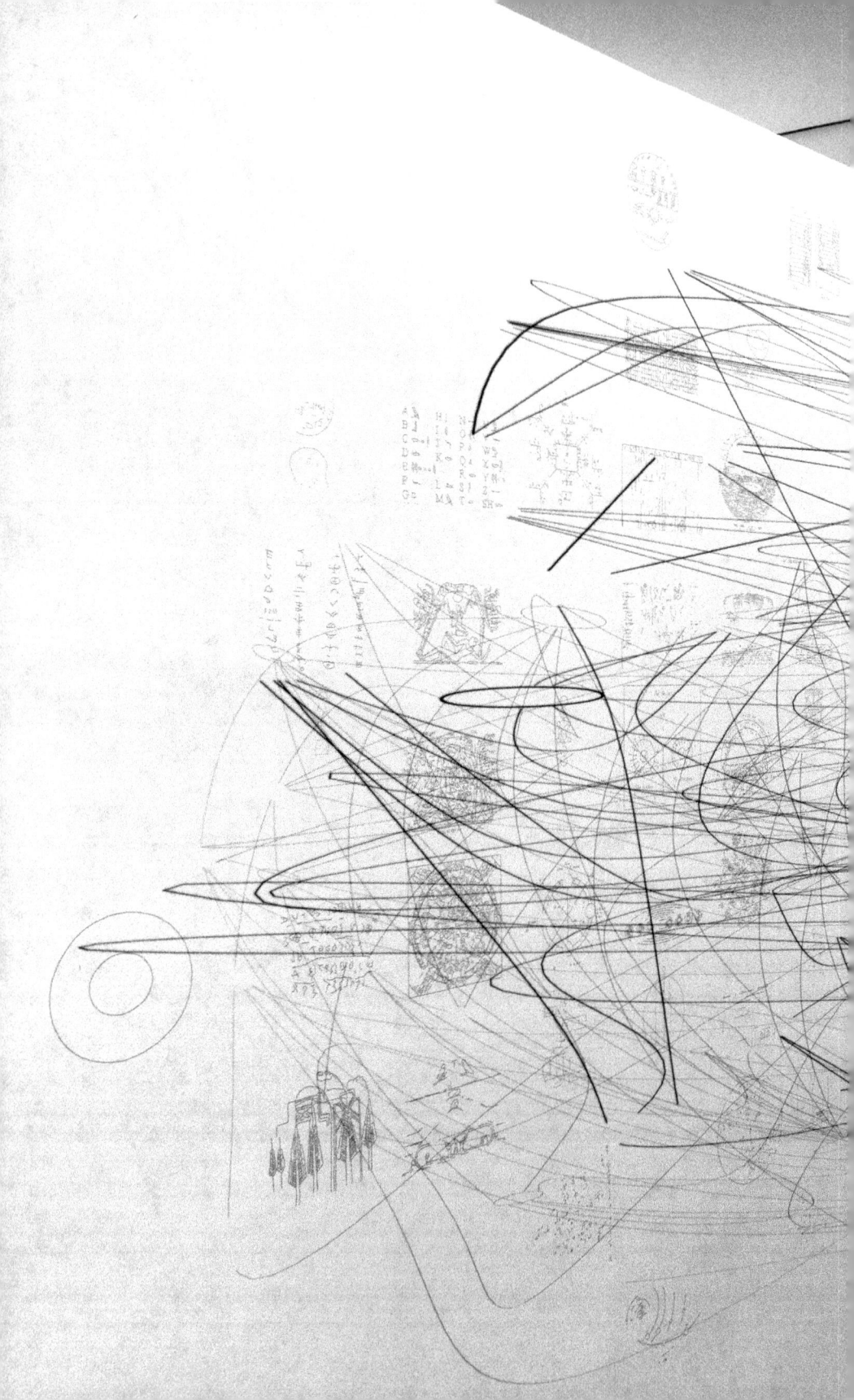

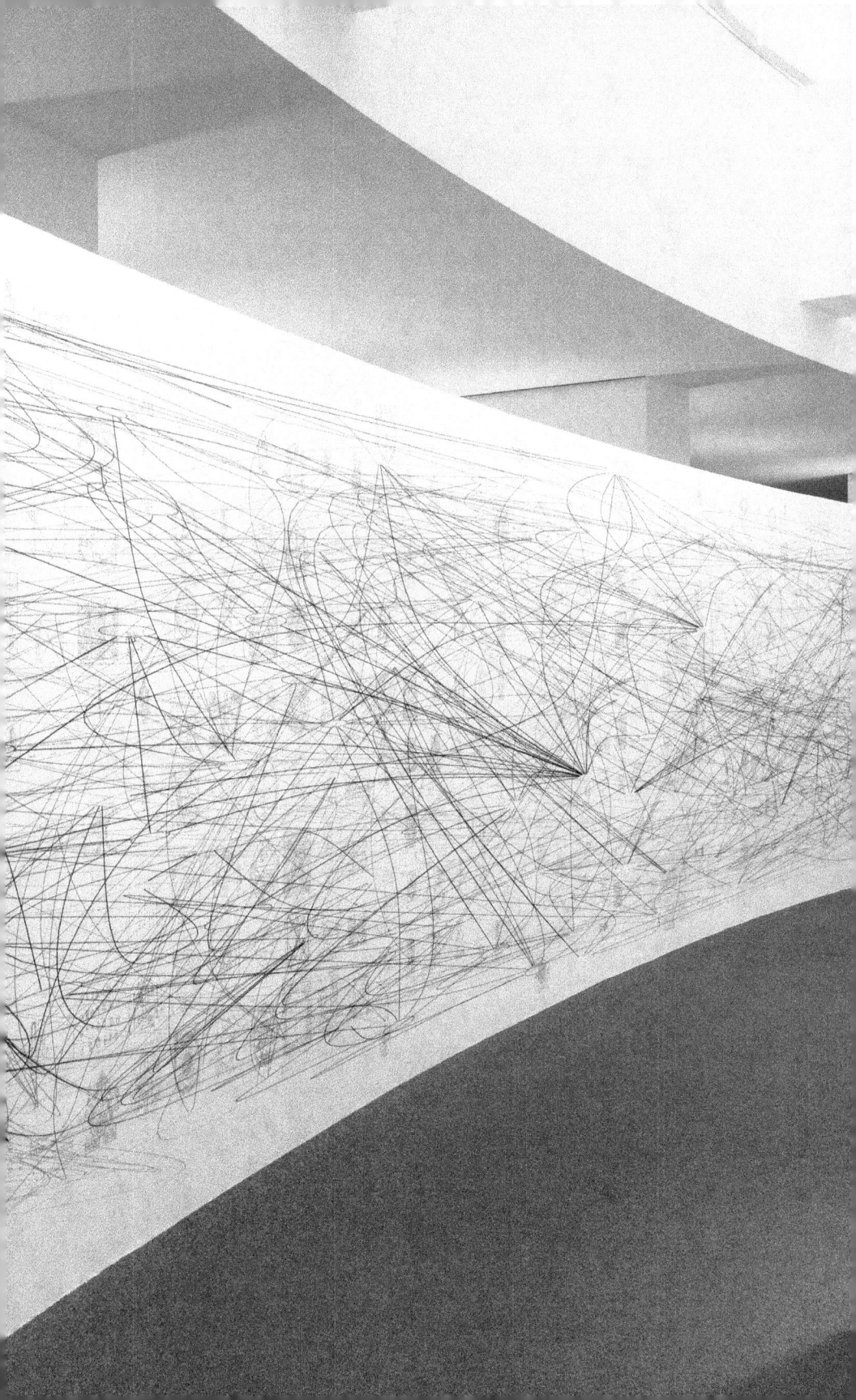

Afterword

In Sanskrit, *bṛh* means "to expand," sometimes magically or miraculously. It is the root of *Bṛahman*—the Absolute Immensity of the All beyond all finite comprehension, the root cause of the cosmos, and the universal creative principle.

In medieval India, *Siddha* of the *Ṛasayana* ("Perfecters" of the "Fluid way," that is, practitioners of Tantric alchemy) applied Bṛahman principle to dictate that by drinking elixirs of mercury and gold, one could not only prolong one's life for centuries, but infinitely expand all time and space.

I first met Matthew Ritchie in 1987 for a brunch at Café Florent on Gansevoort Street in New York City's Meatpacking District. He was with his then girlfriend, now wife, my dear friend Garland Hunter, who wanted me to meet her new boyfriend. Our friendly get-together for a noon brunch expanded into a conversation extending well past sundown and into the late hours, fueled by single malt elixirs. The conversation has extended and expanded ever since (more often without the distillation and imbibing stages of alchemical process).

In spring 2012, Matthew came to the Getty Research Institute as artist-in-residence, and it was one of the great pleasures of my life to assist him on this project where I could, walking through centuries of rare books on physics, philosophy, color theory, chemistry, and alchemy; and poring over emblematic and esoteric symbolism and allegory, cartography, geography, geology, and any number of notions on creation theory, cabinets of wonder, and teratology. Never mind books on perspective and geometry, along with those instructing how to express n-dimensional worlds on the two-dimensional plane of a page.

Many of those images and ideas have found their way into Matthew's artistic expression in this project, manifested in manifold ways. Watching his creative process as the sketches magically expanded in the studio is, and will always be, a fondest memory. I only wish I could perfect the elixir to expand all space and time, so Matthew could have ample working space, and we could continue the conversation as long as we want.

—David Brafman, *Associate Curator, Getty Research Institute*

Artwork © 2017 Matthew Ritchie
Text © 2017 Matthew Ritchie, Kenneth Rogers, and Frederik Stjernfelt for their respective essays
Compilation © 2017 J. Paul Getty Trust

www.ingramcontent.com/pod-product-compliance
Lightning Source LLC
Chambersburg PA
CBHW052320220526
45472CB00001B/203